Heaven Here on Earth

By
Curt Melliger

For permission, serialization, condensation, adaptions, or for our catalog of other publications, write to Ozark Mountain Publishing, Inc., P.O. Box 754, Huntsville, AR 72740, ATTN: Permissions Department.

Library of Congress Cataloging-in-Publication Data

Melliger, Curt – 1956 -
Heaven Here on Earth by Curt Melliger

A Collection of stories about how and where he found Heaven in his travels across the lands.

1. Heaven 2. Religion   3. Metaphysical 4. Spiritual
I. Curt Melliger, 1956 - II. Heaven III. Religion   IV. Metaphysical V. Title

Library of Congress Catalog Card Number: 2018946769
ISBN: 9781940265537

Cover Art and Layout: www.vril8.com
Book set in: Times New Roman, Gabriola
Book Design: Tab Pillar
Published by:

OZARK
MOUNTAIN
PUBLISHING

PO Box 754, Huntsville, AR 72740
800-935-0045 or 479-738-2348; fax 479-738-2448

WWW.OZARKMT.COM

Printed in the United States of America

For Dolores LaChapelle

***

Special thanks to Don and Joyce Downing, Mrs. Jeane Larsen, John Marshall, Deb Getchell, Kim Miller, and Corinne Sandner

***

"What," "Summit of Silver," and "Middle of Night Ode to Joy" originally appeared in *Mountain Gazette*.

"Bridges," "Earth Quakies," and "The Little Girl Who Loved Lilacs" originally appeared in *Durango Telegraph*.

"The Swallow People" originally appeared in *Bird Watcher's Digest*.

"Teacher in a Wheelchair" originally appeared in *Chicken Soup for the Soul*.

"The List" originally appeared in *Oregon Coast*.

Contents

Introduction

The other shore is right here.

—Jack Kerouac

Down through the ages a number of sages have suggested that heaven is actually on earth, or at least available here by way of various means. However, most modern religions have strayed from their beautiful message and instead insist that this current existence is one of sin, suffering, and the curse of possessing a mortal body. They advise us to repent of our wicked nature, reject the pleasures of the flesh, and postpone the ultimate until death allows us to finally approach the divine.

Well, they've got it all wrong. We don't have to wait to experience heaven. Indeed, heaven is waiting for us.

It lurks behind bushes, below bridges, and inside abandoned buildings. It hides on top of high mountains, in deep cool canyons, and at the bottom of the lake. It resides within storm clouds, bolts of lightning, and the colors of a rainbow. It abides on the other side of walls, doors, and stained-glass windows. It exists beneath your feet, behind your back, and in front of your eyelids when they are closed. For paradise is always present, whether we notice it or not.

This book explores how, where, and why heaven is accessible to mere humans. But it is not attained through traditional methods such as doing penance, saying prayers, or paying a steep price. Because, you see, ecstasy is free.

The gates are open.

Curt Melliger
May 7, 2018
Cortez, Colorado

What

What moves the legs when it is no longer I?
What causes me to climb mountains into the sky?
What touches me on the shoulder
just before reaching the summit?
What is that heavenly glow
that I see just above it?
What lends me its strength when I have none left?
What gives me assurance when I should be bereft?
What forces the smile just after I've cried?
What gives me a lift? What gave me a ride?
What stood on the highway, what stood on the shore?
What gives us birth and opens the door?
What sanctions creation instead of destruction?
What gives us smooth sailing instead of obstruction?
What introduced us to our family
what gave us love?
What causes the sunshine to come from above?
What is this thing that set me free
and allows me to see that all is holy?

I do not know
or can not say
writing by a window
full of rain.

Ecstasy in Motion

The word "ecstasy" is usually associated with sex, mind-altering drugs, rock and roll music, skiing bottomless powder, or intense religious experience. But perhaps this ultimate of mortal pleasures is possible through the simple act of doing something we all do each and every day.

Move.

Sadly, it is oftentimes only when we lose the capability to move that we come to comprehend how important, enjoyable, and even ecstatic physical motion actually is. Or, as the old adage concisely states, "You don't know what you got till it's gone."

Most normal, healthy, active people take a great deal for granted. We possess so many abilities, on so many levels, and can so freely and easily go wherever we want that we rarely, if ever, pause and ponder just how wonderful, how magical, how miraculous it is that we are able to move at all. For it is pretty special.

In fact, movement is so very vital to living beings that when it slows and then stops they cease to exist. A bird that injures a wing and can no longer fly through the sky will die on the ground. A horse that breaks a leg and can no longer run will be "put out of its misery." A fish that is removed from water and can no longer swim will perish in a way that is painful to watch. And a plant that no longer receives nourishment from its roots will wilt and wither away into dust on the wind.

While caring for my dying father I learned more about the amazing human body in four months than I had during the previous fifty years. Through numerous discussions with doctors, specialists, and hospice nurses, I began to perceive how the various systems (respiratory, circulatory, digestive, lymphatic, immune, etc.) work together to create a "picture of perfect health" when we are young and strong and capable of doing almost anything.

On the other hand, I also found out how many things can go wrong with the body as it ages, how when the systems do not function in fluid synchronicity with each other they decelerate at an alarming rate and start failing, one by one, as we near our demise. Indeed, when a person slows down to the point where he cannot rise from bed by himself, the final curtain is about to close. Eventually the heart stops beating, the blood quits flowing, and the cessation of all activity signals the end of life.

Therefore, if you are reading this while completely healthy, you should understand that you are living in a state of grace approaching perfection. You currently possess a priceless gift that should not be taken lightly because it can be lost at any moment and might never occur again.

So count your blessings. Count them one by one. Consider them as you stir from a deep slumber, discover yet again that you are still alive, and realize you are now reenergized and raring to jump out of bed and begin your busy day. Contemplate them as you use the bathroom all by yourself, shower without assistance, get dressed, fix breakfast, and chew your food. Appreciate them as you walk out the front door and go to work, or go for a hike, or go on a journey around the world. Celebrate your nearly unlimited advantages, and then reflect upon how the vast majority of them are unavailable without the earthly yet heavenly ability to move.

If you wish to fully fathom the essential importance of physical mobility in human affairs before you grow old, before you falter, before you kick the bucket, I have a few easy—or not so easy—experiments for you to conduct.

First, try standing totally still in one spot for an hour, or half hour, or even five minutes. Notice how the muscles start to cramp, the skin begins to itch, and your entire body aches from the excruciating inactivity. Next, sit in a chair for a lengthy period of time. Feel the back tighten like a torque wrench, the legs go numb as if from cold, and the mind turn to mush from lack of movement. Now lie in bed, in one position, like a cripple, like a comatose patient, like a corpse, for as long as you can, until you cannot tolerate the torture for one more second. Then revel in how utterly delightful it feels to finally turn over, to stretch stiff limbs, to flex sore joints, to hunch the shoulders, to arch the spine like a waking lion, to MOVE.

To join in with the dance once again.

Because, you see, immobility and the lessening of momentum leads to gradual death, while motion and "keeping the ball rolling" offers a life filled with exhilaration. Furthermore, we incredibly lucky human beings are such splendid configurations of almost impossible animation that our mere ability to move somehow allows us to draw near to the divine, to sway with the cosmos, to choreograph our bodies in tune with the flow, the rhythm, the pure and primal sensuality of the living, sentient, never stationary universe that surrounds us like water in the ocean does a swimming sardine.

Yes, the sacred capability to move about, at will, on a whim, on the spur of the moment in any way or fashion or direction we choose is perhaps the most precious present a person could ever receive. If you believe me not, visit a prison, nursing home, veterans' hospital, morgue, or any place where physical activity is severely restricted, limited, or impossible. Then you will begin to understand that the simple yet marvelous act of movement is indeed unadulterated ecstasy.

Especially when you consider the alternative.

Riding the Dragon

Oh golden realm, oh realm of ecstasy,
Where the plumed birds wheel
In the blood red night, oh love,
Tonight, tonight
We shall drink from forbidden fountains.
Come with me.
Let us ride the back of the dragon,
And pull down the moon and the stars ...

—From a Viking poem

When you are hanging onto a tiger you do not wonder how you got there, how you're going to get off, or what you are going to do with the rest of your life if you should somehow, some way survive the ride.

You just hang on.

I have always been attracted to adrenaline rushes. For better or worse, I love those seconds, minutes, and even hours when everything is on the line, the hairs on the nape of my neck rise up and I find myself feeling half scared to death, and yet, curiously, fully alive. Indeed, I am fascinated by those rare events, planned or not, when we are allowed to touch the raw nerve, the main pulse, the primal source of the universe. In other words, I am interested in the place where goosebumps come from.

Call it "riding the dragon."

Remember the tingly feeling you got all over your body riding the fire engine at age six when they suddenly turned the siren on. Recall how it felt to ride a bicycle down the sidewalk all by yourself without Dad holding on. Thrill to the memory of your very first ride on a rollercoaster. And how it felt when you got off ...

Now think what it's like to ride a surfboard on a large moving wave, a raft through raging rapids, a horse at full gallop, a freight train through the Canadian Rockies at age eighteen, a hotrod Camaro across Nebraska at 130 miles an hour.

Of course, doing this sort of thing (i.e., voluntarily leaving the safety net of society) requires your utmost attention, your complete participation, your finest coordination. Therefore, you will need a crystal-clear mind, a sure and steady hand, and nerves of titanium alloy steel. Or none of the above.

One of my first experiences with regular adrenaline rushes came when I was a kid "bombing cars." No, this was nothing like the horrific explosions we hear about in Iraq. Rather, my buddies and I would sneak out at night and throw eggs, tomatoes, rotten apples, snowballs—whatever was in season—at unsuspecting automobiles passing by, and then run like hell when the occasional angry motorist would give chase. We would race down alleys and over fences and through darkened backyards hoping we didn't get caught or arrested or clotheslined by a clothesline. The splendid excitement of our little game was so intoxicating it became addictive, and we loved to brag about our good shots and narrow escapes until the very next time we could go bombing.

With outrageous gleams in our youthful eyes.

Over the ensuing years, I discovered other energizing entertainments to keep my battery charged. There was hitting a baseball with the "sweet spot" of a wooden bat and hearing the roar of the hometown crowd while sprinting around the bases. There was streaking Main Street on a Saturday night as naked as Adam without his fig leaf. There was riding a leaky rowboat down a swollen river during spring flood. There was piloting a railroad track machine along a rickety old branch line at breakneck speed. And there was descending a wet mountain in a lightning storm as fast as my legs could run while every hair on my body was standing straight up (and living to laugh out loud about it crouching in a small cave while a massive hailstorm covered the slope as white as winter in a matter of minutes).

Nothing in life is so exhilarating as to be shot at without result.
—Winston Churchill

I found that I enjoyed exploring the wild places of this planet—the wilder the better. I loved skiing backcountry powder, prowling deserted beaches at dawn, following a cougar's fresh paw prints in the sand, suddenly seeing a bear in the forest, finding bald eagle nests, and peering over the edge of a fearsome towering precipice I had just spent six hours climbing. I relished jumping off a forty-foot cliff into a frigid alpine lake, submerging my body in secluded hot springs and then rolling around in the snow, and staying up all night watching a meteor shower in the desert. I got my kicks doing the wild stuff, the "crazy" stuff, the worthwhile stuff. After so much mediocre.

For we human beings are not meant to settle for the mundane, the ordinary, the merely sufficient. We need the thrill, the excitement, the adrenaline building, building, building until it finally reaches its ultimate and unavoidable climax. Simply put, we need the rush.

Witness the death-defying dance with gravity as the skydiver exits the airplane, the hang glider pushes off from the rim of the mesa, the water skier sails over the jump, the pole vaulter clears twenty feet, and the Acapulco daredevil times his descent to coincide with the incoming wave. See the Olympic downhill racer leaning a tiny bit farther forward than the other skiers, nailing every turn, smoking every straightaway, and winning the gold medal by one-tenth of one-tenth of a second. Observe the ice skater as she performs a flawless routine from opening flourish to final bow. Hear Eric Clapton take off on a soaring solo and not let up until he gets it "just right."

Listen to the Alleluia Chorus at full volume.

Now watch someone run the table in 8-ball, pitch a no-hitter in baseball, or bowl a perfect game. Watch the fearless young men ride the bull, the bucking bronco, the kayak over a waterfall, the rappel down an overhanging cliff, the Pipeline curl on a monster day. Watch them leap from high bridges with only a bungee cord attached to their ankles.

Think about Charles Lindbergh crossing the Atlantic Ocean for the very first time in an airplane, Edmund Hillary and Tenzing Norgay climbing Mount Everest in 1953, John Glenn circling the earth in a tin can, Evel Knievel attempting to jump the Snake River Gorge on a rocket-powered motorcycle, and the tightrope artist calmly walking between two skyscrapers. All without a safety net.

Indeed, there are so many risky, hazardous, almost-suicidal things that we humans don't "have" to do, but we do them anyway. Why? Because we can. Because they are such fun. Because we love breaking rules, dodging bullets, and getting away with murder. Because surviving a ride on a tiger is one of the finest gifts we could ever receive.

Now, these unforgettable experiences are readily available on this incredible planet of ours, but only if we are willing to take a chance, a little trip, a magic carpet ride, an occasional walk on the wild side. To do this, all that is necessary is a love of adventure, a healthy dose of pure adrenaline, and perhaps a change of underwear.

Do not shy away from these worthy activities, these excellent options, these exhilarating opportunities for enlightenment. Because, you see, life is short and death is long, and we must discover, we must enjoy, we must appreciate the best, the finest, the ultimate stuff while we still can. Or, as they say in the Wasatch Mountains on a powder morning, "Sleep when you're dead."

Yes, there is much to be gained from riding the back of the dragon, the edge of the razor blade, the nose of the rocket. But perhaps the greatest wonder of all is the fact that when life is moving so deliriously fast, you don't *have time* to realize the present danger until the rollercoaster ride is finally over and you arrive safely on the other side of eternity, none the worse for wear.

Because you do not think about broken bones when you are skiing the trees. You do not worry about health insurance while carving a wave that could crush you if you fall. And you never, ever ask why you are climbing so high on a mountain that reaches halfway into the sky.

You just do it.

For we human beings tend to forget about normal things, usual reasons, possible excuses, potential perils, and impending disaster while we are living life to the fullest.

Summit of Silver

The world seems made of mountains; a chaotic mass of rocky ridges, peaks and spurs.

—William N. Byers, on first recorded ascent of LaPlata Peak, Colorado, July 26, 1873

People have all kinds of reasons for climbing high mountains. Most of them are good ones, others not so much. Some folks do it for the exercise, the cardiovascular workout, the healthy way the human body feels after steady and prolonged exertion at high elevation. Some do it for the adventure, or the challenge, perhaps even the risk factor, whereby a little bit of potential danger is allowed into one's safe and sheltered and boring existence. Other people climb mountains to prove something to themselves, or to impress their friends, or for bragging rights. Checklists, ego trips, and stories at the office on Monday morning. Peak baggers, posers, and wannabes. Still others have purer motives. "To reach the top." To enjoy the view. To experience the beauty. To commune with Mother Nature. To visit with the mountain gods. They climb because they are young, and wild, and able to. Because climbing is in their blood. "Because it's there."

Touché. Bravo. Und wunderbar.

However, while I can certainly relate to some of these motivations, my main justification for climbing high peaks is somewhat different than all of the above. For, you see, my number one reason for ascending is perhaps the simplest of them all. I just want to go to Heaven. Which, as far as I can tell, is way, WAY up there.

And so I climb, and go to the top of the mountain, the very topmost point, therefore to get as close to Heaven while still on earth as is humanly possible. As often as I can. Well, okay, maybe not so much anymore. But there was a time in my life, a good, long time, when I got high—real high—on a regular basis. And so it was in the breakaway summer of 1994 ...

The previous few months had not been pleasant. All at once, it seemed, I was injured at work, lost a good job, broke up with my girlfriend (whose house I was living at), and found myself homeless. I was bouncing around from place to place, trying to recuperate, and furthermore attempting to figure out "what to do" with the rest of my life, or at least the next chapter. So then, as spring turned into summer and my health was gradually returning, I decided to take a break from society and spend the season up in the mountains, alone, camping out, and climbing everything I possibly could.

I started slow, rebuilding my mountain legs by doing thousand-foot ascents and moderate hikes in the foothills. Little by little, I once again graduated to the twelves, and thirteens, and then the fourteeners. I would park my truck in some nice out-of-the-way place at 9 or 10,000 feet, get up early in the morning, and "go and see the Wizard" (as I called it).

Weather permitting, I would summit several peaks per week, sometimes a couple in one day. The Elks, the Raggeds, the Collegiate Range, the Sawatch, the San Juans became my new home.

The air is clear and thin. As you climb, breathe easily and make the natural adjustments in your body. Feel the slow change in yourself. Think of climbing up as a downward flow, without strain...

—Tai Chi master

My lungs expanded, thigh muscles hardened, skin turned brown, and the new mountaineering boots broke in quickly. I fine-tuned my camping routine, firewood skills, and eye for beauty. I often stayed away from people for a week or more at a time. I learned, or rather relearned how to move like an animal, and walk quietly, and time my breathing with my steps, and touch things with respect, and take only what was needed. Kneeling at the shrine. Sucking on the nipple. Learning to live again.

Which brought me, finally, one dark and stormy morning, to LaPlata Peak, the fifth-highest summit in Colorado.

Actually, the weather wasn't bad early on. Leaving the trailhead at 10,000 feet, I could see several patches of blue sky overhead. "Sucker holes," they're called. Heading south up LaPlata Gulch, I passed numerous waterfalls and delightful pools of crystal-clear water on the side of the mountain. Filling my canteens from the creek at 11,200 feet, I then ascended straight east up a rocky couloir following numerous trail switchbacks that were only twenty feet apart. Reaching the northwest ridge of LaPlata Peak at 12,700 feet, I was promptly greeted by a stiff southeast wind and a great view of Mount Elbert (highest point in Colorado) and Ellingwood Ridge (a famous, jagged, impossibly rugged wall of rock stretching far to the north) and, well, that was about it. For the impending storm had begun to lower, thicken, and fill in the holes, and soon, very soon, even Elbert and Ellingwood were lost in the swirling grayness.

Having experienced way too many lightning storms at high altitude, I always try to be keenly aware of any thunder or electrical energy when above timberline, both present and potential. On this day, luckily, there was none, and I felt relatively safe as I climbed due south on steep, green-lichened stone past old gray snowfields from last winter. The clouds enveloped the entire mountain like an old wet blanket and began to drizzle. Soon the drizzle turned into a sprinkle, then rain, then sleet, and then snow, but I just kept going up, and up, and up. First tracks, indeed. Having earlier passed four other climbers who were headed down, down to avoid the coming storm, I was most likely the only person on the upper part of the peak.

(Note: The summit register inside the old mailbox on top had been signed by thirty-eight people the previous day when the weather was sunny and bluebird.)

Then, just as I was ascending the final section, and nearing the lofty silver summit in a driving wet summer blizzard, something funny happened to me. Or in me. Or all around me.

It had been a long hard climb, and the weather was getting worse every minute, but I was bound and determined to reach the top. This was the highest mountain I had ever climbed in this lifetime, and normally I would have been tired, hungry, and looking forward to relaxing on the summit. However, on this particular day, in a raging August snowstorm, at fourteen thousand feet, something else occurred within me. Something else entirely.

For, as I scaled the final arête, and could see the stone cairn indicating the apex of the huge massif that I had just spent five hours climbing, a profound sense of sadness suddenly came over me! Instead of the deep satisfaction normally experienced upon reaching the top of a high mountain, I actually felt, somehow, bummed out. Indeed, I was downright disappointed at having reached the summit, which had now become the finish line, the end of the trail, the uppermost limit of this climb. As in, "Here's the summit already, damn it, I wish this ridge just kept right on going up and up and up, I want to go higher and higher and higher and just keep climbing into the clouds, ALL THE WAY, my goal is not this here mere pile of rocks, no, no, my goal is up there, somewhere up there, still up there, way up there, why oh why do I have to stop here at 14,361 feet?"

It was like I had been climbing the final, last, most important stairway of them all, the one that goes to Heaven itself, but suddenly, much too soon, the steps seemed to stop here. Right here. Just when I was getting close!

The wind was out of the south now, so I dropped back down over the north face a ways to escape the driving wet snow. I put on my last layer of clothes, found a place to ride out the storm, and ate my lunch like a larva in its cocoon.

Then, later, as I was sipping my customary summit can of cold Budweiser, the snow began to let up, the wind died down, and eventually, slowly but surely, the wonderful, wonderful sun came out. Oh happy day …

The storm clouds lowered and started to dissipate into thin air, while enormous mountains, and then groups of mountains, began to appear as if by magic, sheer magic, in all directions, distances, and elevations, like a sea of endless and thus eternal waves rising up and out of the misty nothingness. My wide-opened eyes reveled in every new look that I took. Sun and clouds danced with each other, both down below and up above me. The constant interplay of shadow and light altered the mystical tapestry with each passing moment. I literally could not stop seeing new summits, ridges, canyons, lakes, and even whole ranges wherever my eyes would gaze. The Gores to the north, the Mosquitoes, the Collegiates, and Pike's Peak. The Sangre de Cristos, Uncompahgres, Chinese Mountains, and Sopris. The West Elks, Flat Tops, Mount Massive and, once again, Mount Elbert, shining in the sun like a castle made of porcelain.

Etcetera.

It seemed I could see half of Colorado all spread out in front of me, behind me, indeed all around me, when just an hour earlier I could barely see two steps ahead. The high-elevation post-storm sunlight was so warm and so intense that the fresh white snow was literally evaporating before my very eyes and rising in veils of silver steam back up into the blue, blue sky from whence it had recently come.

While laying out my wet clothes to dry in the brilliant solar heat, I felt a sense of peace come over me. A serenity from some source much greater than myself welled up within me, and I felt like I had finally made it home. Home, sweet home, at last.

My earlier sadness, worry, and injury were now gone, gone for good. I was healed. And now knew "what to do" …

After spending three hours of pure unadulterated rapture on the very top of LaPlata Peak, I had to practically force myself to leave. Because, you see, I wanted to just remain there and never, ever depart. But I simply could not stay up there forever. Could I?

Just before heading down, I looked around one final time. All of a sudden, I could scarcely believe my eyes! Because it was then, then that I realized why the sacred staircase through the storm clouds up to Heaven had stopped here, right here at this high and holy place.

For I had reached my destination, after all.

Thank You Times Three

In *The Scripture of the Golden Eternity*, Jack Kerouac describes a strikingly blissful experience he had one day while alone in his yard. It seems the author was on the ground sniffing some flowers, and when he stood up the blood rushed into his head and he "fainted, or died" for about a minute.

As he lay there in the grass on his back, he was given a glorious vision of "the golden eternity," including a brief glimpse of Heaven. He found himself suddenly understanding "the joyful mysterious essence of Arrangement" and comprehending "where it all came from and where it is all returning." Near the end of this stunning piece, Jack is clearly running out of words to explain the beatific ecstasy available here on earth, so he finishes by coming straight to the point: "O thank you thank you thank you."

Over the years this short yet powerful phrase has stuck to me like Superglue. I use it often, both consciously and unconsciously, both out loud and silently, both in public and when completely alone. I use it to express my dumbfounded appreciation for some small or huge stroke of luck, some insignificant or magnificent gift, some obvious or almost invisible godsend. I use it every time something comes my way and makes my day, as I then expose it to the bright light of awareness through the simple act of acknowledging it by articulating the magic words. Because, you see, "Oh thank you, thank you, thank you" has now become an all-purpose prayer to me. It is a chant, a poem, a haiku, a song, a hymn of praise. It is a blessing, a benediction, an invocation, a momentary meditation on the meaning of existence, and a favorite bell that I like to ring on a regular basis.

It is the gift that is always returnable.

Furthermore, this repetitive yet strangely potent saying has evolved into my muse's way of reminding me to honor not only the big stuff of this world but the tiny entities as well. For we are provided with so much—so much!—in this life, every day, every night, every minute, every single second of consciousness, even while we sleep. We are given to, we receive from, and, hopefully, we offer it back. Or as the old biker slogan states, "What goes around comes around."

In other words, give the gift away. Do not keep it for yourself. Return it to where it came from. Repay the favor by showing your heartfelt gratitude. For there are so very many things to say "thank you" for.

Just look at all of the ones most of us normally take for granted. The waking up each morning, the lightbulb coming on yet again, the resumption of daily animation. The ability to get out of bed. The blessings of a steadily beating heart, constantly flowing blood, and continually breathing lungs. The miracle of eyes that see and ears that hear and skin that feels and a tongue that speaks and a spirit that soars like a California condor.

The presents of desert and ocean, mountain and canyon, full moon and rainfall, family and friends. Sunshine during the day and starlight late at night, hot chocolate on a chilly morning and ice-cold drinks on a sultry afternoon, rainbow trout splashing in the stream and a swarm of swallows pirouetting in the sky, laughter and kindness, good health and passion, autumn colors and winter fire, spring thaw and summer garden. Good food and fine conversation and having fun, skiing and swimming and walking to the store, memory and magic, perfection and grace. The heavenly voice of Eva Cassidy, the inspired poetry of Pattiann Rogers, the impeccable paintings of Robert Arnold, the "spontaneous prose" of Kerouac, the lyrical waterfalls of Dolores LaChapelle. And so on and so forth. Etcetera.

Yes, the roster of things to be grateful for is almost endless. We could spend the rest of our lives writing them down and still not finish the list before we die. And if we were to verbally say "thank you" for each and every one of them, we would not only eventually wear out our vocal chords but also grow weary of hearing the hallowed words.

So don't say thanks for everything. But be sure to say it every day, at least once, even if only upon waking, even if only before eating supper, even if it is only audible to any angels who may be listening.

For when you are truly thankful you are filled with thanksgiving, you are infused with comprehension, you are saturated with a sincere appreciation of where it is that gifts ultimately come from. Indeed, you might even sense the presence of God—the real one who needs no religion—whenever you say the sacred phrase, whether it be out loud or just to yourself. For the soul, the essence, the holiness, the nature, the grandeur, the pure unadulterated JOY of being alive is closely associated with an attitude of gratitude, of being beholden, of noticing our numerous blessings and then counting them, one by one.

Because by showing gratefulness for the little things of this universe, we are demonstrating our relationship with something much larger.

Through the Rainbow

Human beings are so very lucky. For somehow we mere mortals are yet surrounded by miracles, by evidence of the divine, by undeniable proof of something far grander than ourselves. Indeed, we are perpetually encircled by marvels and mysteries, flashes of light and glimpses of glory, accessible ecstasies and possibly even a few passageways into heaven itself. So it is with rainbows.

One time years ago, I was hiking in a deep, steep, normally shaded canyon of the Colorado River shortly after an afternoon shower. As the atmosphere was clearing in the west, the area around me became "colorized," as if the very air molecules had been suddenly transformed into tiny crystals reflecting sunlight. Everything was now glowing in fantastic colors, in every hue imaginable, and furthermore infused with a rich velvet bell-ringing goldness that reminded me of long ago.

Rounding a bend in the river, I came upon a full double rainbow spanning the gorge from rock wall to rock wall. The arrangement of incredibly vivid colors in parallel rows ran the entire spectrum from dark purple to neon blue to electric green to immaculate yellow to Day-Glo orange to brilliant red to shimmering violet. The world and sky seemed to meet and mate in perfect harmony within the arc of the rainbow, as if the soaring arch of bedazzling light were a crack in the mirror of reality allowing me to see a glimmer of the sacred place that resides on the vast endless other side of this small and imperfect one we currently inhabit.

Standing there with my mouth involuntarily open in awe, it occurred to me that rainbows are the bridge in between heaven and earth, an ethereal yet visible thread connecting the two. Perhaps even a hint of things to come.

Since that blessed day in Glenwood Canyon—a "peak experience" for sure—I have witnessed many other instances of rainbows in this realm, and not only the obvious ones manifested across the firmament like fireworks that make us go "Wow." For example, see the rainbow colors leaping from the icicle, the stream, the gleam in a bubble of sea foam. See them materialize in the mist of a waterfall, the spray of a lawn sprinkler, the droplets of morning dew on a spiderweb in the weeds. See them glistening in pigeon feathers, butterfly wings, and the scales of a freshly caught rainbow trout. Notice the rainbow in the sunrise, the sunset, the northern lights at night, the "sun dogs" that circle the summer sun, the "mare's tail" clouds that parade through the heavens permeated with pink, turquoise, and aquamarine, in the newly fallen snowflakes when a break in the storm creates a million crystals of sheer visual delight.

However, not all rainbow images are provided by Mother Nature. A number of excellent ones were invented by man. Observe the bright colors emanating from the sun catcher, the cut diamond, the optical prism, the camera lens, the chrome bumper, the Christmas tree lights, the freshly frosted windowpane of winter.

Now watch them emerge like magic in the most humble and lowly of locations. Perceive the refraction, reflection, and dispersion of the sun's rays in places like junkyards, parking lots, and puddles of stagnant water. I kid you not.

In fact, one of the most stunning sights in all of creation is the supremely concentrated palette of hues produced when gas leaks from a car's fuel line, lands in a pool of water, and is touched just so by sunlight like Vincent Van Gogh with a psychedelic paintbrush. Such a lush and lustrous kaleidoscope of silken smooth colors unexpectedly comes to life as the dirty old gasoline mixes, or rather doesn't mix, with the plain blank medium of water. Swirling rivers of pure silver and flaming orange and blazing scarlet and beaming-from-within green and ocean submarine blue and Martian marshmallow purple flow gently in super slow motion across the pavement, the colors so shiny, so vibrant, so exquisitely *clean* in spite of the contaminated canvas. It's like a rainbow spilling right down here on earth, a fluorescent flag unfurling, an ever-growing, constantly changing, utterly fascinating work of contemporary art far beyond any human form, indeed a veritable mural of paradise incarnate being gradually exposed on the parking lot cement.

The way the gasoline glides and shimmies and twirls in the water puddle, the way it develops into distinct stripes and streaks and patterns of infinite resplendence is akin to watching a Technicolor movie in broad daylight, or tripping on psilocybin, or beholding God's paint can as it tips over on the floor. For to me, the unintentional merging of gas with water and sunshine is nothing less than a keyhole into the fabulous mystery of life, into the inner essence of all this gloom, which of course is ecstasy. It is the suddenly unhidden secret, the slightly open window, the seam in between this world and the one we originate from and long to return to. The "dark light" of Tao revealed in oh-so-living color.

Perfection for free, if we see.

Yes, something as simple and mundane as a fuel spill in filthy water can yet deliver an important message from the other side of the curtain, which is that our lovely home planet and heaven itself are not far apart.

Perhaps paradise lies not only "over the rainbow" as the old song suggests, but also below.

The Blood of Earth

If there is magic on this planet, it is contained in water.
—Loren Eiseley

As a young boy growing up in eastern Nebraska I was endlessly fascinated by water, especially when it was in motion. I loved to watch the way the strange, mysterious, almost invisible liquid would flow out of the faucet at the turn of a handle, fill a cup, spill over the rim, and disappear down the drain. I enjoyed wading in cool streams and shallow rivers, sensing the inherent holiness of the gentle yet powerful element that was caressing my legs, each and every molecule moving in exquisite harmony with all of the others.

I liked how water felt on my skin, how it tingled when it slid off my body, how it swirled around in the swimming pool. I reveled in the sounds of water, the dripping, lapping, splashing noises, the almost-silent movement of a wave. I was spellbound by the dazzling Day-Glo colors that water produced when reflecting light; I was enthralled by how the thicker layers displayed a luminous blue hue similar to the sky; I was tickled pink whenever I bent over a puddle and my face would magically appear in the mirror. I was exhilarated by thunder, by lightning, by rainy mornings, by stormy nights, by torrential downpours and the threat of flash flood from the nearby Wolf River.

Yes, there was something scary yet comforting, mundane yet mesmerizing, supernatural yet eminently earthly about this slick, shiny, velvety smooth substance known as "water," and I had to get to the bottom of it.

While most people, parents and playmates alike, despised wet weather, I was different. I prayed for rain. I did rain dances in the garden. To me there was nothing more thrilling than the sky slowly darkening, the clouds swelling up like pregnant purple monsters, and the energy level rising astronomically just before they released their payday, their manna, their heavenly ecstasy in the form of raindrops, first just a few, then a pitter-patter, then a barrage that would pound the roof of our house, race into aluminum gutters, then freefall through the downspout and come gushing out onto the grass, dispersing like diamonds across the yard.

I would spend the gloomy, gleeful, rainy days of my youth chasing the elusive liquid wherever it went, which I soon discovered was down, down, always down. Constantly descending, constantly obeying the law of gravity, constantly searching for someplace enchanted like the gray washtub behind Grandma's house, or a small lake developing in the deserted park, or a street quickly becoming a stream, or a steel storm drain where tiny angels could be heard tinkling the keys of a subterranean piano. Following the dancing, prancing, gallivanting rain became my fondest delight, and I never tired of watching the water form creeks and rapids and waterfalls on its voyage, on its pilgrimage, on its ever-ongoing journey home.

Some things never change, and fifty years later I am still captivated by moving water. Indeed, as time goes by it has become even more and more beguiling to me, instead of fading away as usually happens to the simple pleasures and ethereal joys of childhood as we reach maturity. Because, you see, water is special. More special, it seems, than toys and games and make-believe. For water is real, it is lasting, it is forever, like the sky, like the heavens, like Heaven itself.

> *The rain-filled bucket*
> *Brimming with beautiful water.*
> —Santōka Taneda

Water is a common theme in Oriental literature, often used to symbolize calmness, humility, and the pathway to understanding. For water—plain old H_2O—is important. In fact, essential. Maybe even magic.

Much can be learned from the observation of water. Notice its many unique abilities and exceptional qualities. For instance, water can be as hard and unbreakable as ice, or as soft and ephemeral as a droplet of morning dew on a spider's web. It can come pouring and roaring off a high cliff in a mighty cascade that crashes into the whirlpool below, or it can rise and float, silently and unseen, back up into the cloud from whence it once descended. A glass of cold water on a hot humid afternoon can go down your throat into your stomach and emerge from your skin as sweat and soak your T-shirt, thereby cooling you twice. Water can take the form of steam, fog, mist, drizzle, rain, sleet, snowflakes, or six-foot icicles hanging like Christmas decorations from the eaves. It can make your breath visible during winter. It can produce booming rumbles of thunder, soothing "white noise" at the beach, double rainbows after a shower, flower gardens in the desert, and hot springs in the frigid mountains. It provides a coolant for friction, a boiler for food, a medium for surfers, champagne powder for skiers, and a protective cushion for a baby in his mother's belly.

Water cooled this fiery planet, made it inhabitable, and created the Garden of Eden we still see before us today. Indeed, water was the first spark, the initial contact from above, the igniting of life's volcano. It is the main ingredient, for which there is no substitute.

Water feeds us, nourishes us, sustains us all from the womb until the tomb. It lubricates our bodies, stimulates our minds, invigorates our spirit. It cleans what is dirty, heals what is sore, softens what is hard, moistens what is dry, loosens what is stuck, satisfies what is thirsty, saves what is dying, and gives life to what has none.

One of water's most intriguing aspects is its tendency to yield to everything that confronts it, and yet win in the end. For example, water is gentle, and rock is not. Water gives, rock doesn't. And yet, as the ancient proverb proves, "water carves rock."

In other words, water is the softest, most supple, most yielding substance in the universe, and yet it has no equal in destruction. For something so seemingly weak and submissive can still turn steel into rust, stone into dust, and an entire crop into ruin during a ten-minute hail storm. It can wreck your house, it can rip out a dam, it can flood a valley, it can sculpt a Grand Canyon, it can submerge an island, it can flatten a mountain range.

And yet, on the other hand, something so destructive has no equal in creation. For water is the ultimate incubator, the genesis, perhaps even the source of all existence, all organisms, all living and sentient beings. It has aided in developing every wonder that we witness on this wonder-filled planet, this oasis in space, this paradise incarnate. For water is the river, the river of life, the giver of life. It

21

is "the drink that refreshes," indeed, the finest elixir of them all, with the smell, taste, and texture of eternity.

The cup
of cool water
waits patiently
for your lips.

The Tao Te Ching, a Chinese scripture from 500 BC, suggests that we humans imitate the characteristics of water if we wish to become happy, fulfilled, enlightened souls. For the author, Lao Tzu, noticed that heaven is actually *on earth*. It is not specifically "up there," or "in the hereafter," or something that can be achieved through the doing of good deeds, the obeying of commandments, or the reciting of prayers. Because, you see, heaven is free, and simple, and available, right here. As is water. So if you want to get to heaven, watch how water behaves.

Follow it around for awhile. See where it goes, which is down to earth, down to the ground, down to the very bottom of the barrel, before it eventually evaporates, is lifted up into the sky, and returns to the wellspring.

Learn from water. Be like water. Helpful and selfless, humble and lowly, fluid and fearless. Plain, yet brilliant. Calm, yet quick. Soft, yet powerful. Strong, yet gentle. Yielding, yet indestructible.

Look to nature for advice. Search earth and sky for the wisdom of the ages. Discover the secret, the miracle of life, the lifeblood of this planet, the envy of the entire cosmos, the liquid form of God revealed right in front of our eyes.

At the turn of a faucet handle.

For if what is magic, if what is sacred, if what is necessary for animation be the question, water is the answer.

Bridges

You know the greatest thing in life? It's to almost die.
To do something where you almost go over the edge but
you don't, but you get a glimpse of the edge.
—Ted Nugent

I'm sitting underneath the bridge that crosses the LaPlata River a half-mile south of my house. A peaceful, cool, delightful spot. It reminds me of other bridges I have known and sat under. Other places that I have been. Other realms of mystery and wonder.

Most people who drive over this humble little span never think twice about it, never imagine what's beneath, never speculate on who built it, never notice how high or low the water is, never see the deer and red fox that come here in the morning. They never visit on a warm summer afternoon, and sit in the cool shade, and look at the beautiful things to be seen, and watch the neon colors in the stream, and listen to the magical tinkling noises that the water makes. Like music from another lifetime.

Underneath the bridge there are weeds and rocks, bird nests and spiderwebs, steel girders and angel voices, secret places where wild animals live, and golden reflections in the water of a world upside-down. As if Heaven were below, not above.

I have always liked bridges. Even as a child. Especially as a child. An early photograph shows me standing in front of a huge, tall bridge. I'm about four years old, posing confidently on the edge of a rocky cliff overlooking the Royal Gorge in Colorado, with the imposing structure that spans it just behind me. In this old black-and-white picture, taken by my father while on family vacation, I look very content. Indeed, I seem right at home among the high mountains and deep canyons and towering pine trees, even though I grew up on the prairie of eastern Nebraska, which was a good place to grow up because we had lots of bridges.

There were several creeks, wonderful creeks, and two rivers, the Loup and the Platte. So us boys naturally spent a lot of our free time investigating these waterways and the bridges that crossed them. Highway bridges, county road bridges, railroad bridges, farmer bridges, abandoned bridges. We enjoyed climbing around on the bigger ones, and exploring underneath the smaller ones. Looking for hidden treasure. Searching for stuff. And finding it.

I learned early on that not many people hang out at bridges. Usually just kids. And teenage hoodlums. And hobos. And fishermen. And bridge workers. And wandering poets. All of whom I get along with. All of whom I have been.

Some things never change. And I still love bridges. Literally and metaphorically. Steel bridges, wooden bridges, and cement bridges. Viaducts, overpasses, and catwalks. Footbridges, logs across streams, and stepping-stones. Bridges over rivers and canals and dry arroyos. Bridges that take you from one place to another, one state to another, one country to another. From a normal frame of mind to a different point of view. Bridges that teach you a whole new way of life …

While in my twenties I worked on a bridge crew for the Rio Grande Railroad in western Colorado. Although we also took care of the buildings, crossings, tunnels, etc., I most enjoyed working on the bridges. Especially the big tall bridges spanning wild rapid rivers, where I would spend my days climbing around on steel girders and huge timbers, just like when I was a kid.

However, one time, while we were re-decking a bridge high over the Roaring Fork River, I made a bad mistake and almost met my demise. One false step, just one, and I suddenly felt myself falling, falling through the bridge. I thought I was going to go the whole sixty feet to the rocks below.

Then time slowed down. Indeed, it seemed to stand still.

You have heard stories of people seeing their lives pass in front of their eyes just before they die. Well, I didn't see my entire life, but I did witness parts of it, passing in front of my eyes, in slow motion, and in great detail, as I fell to my death. As it were, I saw plenty.

However, luck was with me that day, and I did not perish. For, supporting this long steel span over the river canyon were two lofty cement piers. And where I fell through just happened to be directly over one of them, so I dropped only ten feet, instead of all the way.

I was alive.

I was alive, but something had changed during my abbreviated flight. Indeed, I not only saw parts of my past during the fall, but decided what to do with my future if I should somehow, miraculously, survive the impossible. Which I did.

That bridge transformed my life. And, in spite of my near-death experience, I still like high bridges. And always will. I guess it's only natural.

Because I have always loved good viewpoints, and deep cool canyons, and the sound of moving water. And crazy, ecstatic, mysterious places where nobody else ever goes. Except for kids, and bums, and other souls interested in Heaven.

Which is right here. Right down here on earth. How do I know that Heaven is on earth? Because I found it.

Underneath this bridge.

Upon Awakening

I saw the sun ... I realized I was neither dead nor in Hell.
I felt life stirring inside me ...
And suddenly I could move and speak again.
—Martha N., patient at Mount Carmel Hospital, 1969

It is interesting to note the mood, mind frame, and speech pattern of a person upon waking from a state of profound unconsciousness. Whether the episode be perfectly normal such as a deep sleep, ecstatic such as a heavenly vision, or traumatic such as a brain injury-induced coma spanning half a lifetime, the subject will often reveal intimate details of this ever-mysterious realm we inhabit through his uninhibited behavior and semiconscious vocalizations in much the same way the very first rays of the rising sun are always the brightest ones.

For example, notice how you feel in the morning after eight hours of peaceful slumber. Savor the sense of being fully rested, the resultant mental clarity, the sheer energy bubbling over from within, the urge to take on the coming day. Now compare this to your experience when you awaken from a powerful dream, whether it be good or bad.

First the good. There you are lying in bed while slowly returning from a nocturnal visit to paradise. You wish you could stay there forever, but you can not. And yet somehow you manage to remain on the other side of the wall for several rapturous minutes, as reality has difficulty chasing the angels away.

Now the bad. Remember the awful outlook on life you had after "coming to" following a full-blown freaking nightmare where all of your worst dreams apparently came true. As you lay there recoiling in a half-conscious/half-unconscious state you find yourself embracing reality like never before, if only to hasten the bizarre images back into the blackness where they came from.

Obviously there is much to be learned from our nighttime adventures while deeply submerged in REM sleep, not to mention our immediate reactions and initial thoughts upon emerging and regaining sensibility. Indeed, there is a tribe in southeast Asia that gathers around the campfire each morning to share their dreams with one another and examine them thoroughly, beginning with the youngest children first.

On a related note, primitive societies often treated people suffering from epilepsy in one of two distinctly different fashions. Either they were regarded as emissaries of the gods and therefore greatly revered, or they were deemed to be possessed by demons and promptly killed. The favored ones were closely observed by doctors during their violent seizures for any omens they might display. Afterward, when the spell was broken, the patient would be interviewed by elders to see if there was a message from beyond the veil being conveyed to their tribe.

Similarly, a boxer who is knocked out not only sustains a concussion and at least some brain damage, but also undergoes a "mini coma" and may exhibit some of the after-effects of a longer one. Boxing coaches carefully monitor a fighter's behavior when he regains consciousness following a KO, because how he reacts to his involuntary nap may indicate not only how much harm was done, but also how he will be affected in the long run. For instance, if he sits up in the ring and says, "Where's the s.o.b. who hit me?" that is considered a healthy sign. However, if he shows any fright upon waking, his pugilistic career may be over.

In his remarkable book *Awakenings*, Dr. Oliver Sacks describes his work at a New York City hospital with patients suffering from the notorious "sleeping sickness" epidemic of 1916–1927.

Some of them were completely comatose, some semicomatose, still others severely disabled by a wide variety of disturbing dementias, involuntary spasms, and unstoppable tics. The people in perpetual comas were effectively "petrified," both physically and mentally, as if they were statues of stone instead of human beings made of flesh and bone. Yet their hearts were still beating, their lungs still breathing, their status still listed as "living," even if only barely so. One physician referred to them as "insubstantial as ghosts"; another as "extinct volcanoes."

Then in 1969 (coinciding with the "Summer of Love" sweeping across America) Dr. Sacks and his staff at Mount Carmel began experimenting with a promising new drug known as L-DOPA. His description of the "awakenings" on his ward is nothing short of astonishing. Although scholarly in tone, full of unfamiliar terms (the glossary comes in handy), and occasionally heartbreaking (only a small percentage of the patients were permanently cured), this book is nonetheless an eloquent and touching tribute to the loveliness and resiliency of the human spirit.

Try—if you can—to imagine what those people must have experienced when they awoke from their debilitating condition and returned to the land of the conscious, the feeling, the mobile, the aware, the *alive*—the world of the senses!—even if only for a few precious months, or weeks, or just days in some cases. As the previously comatose patients came back to existence after being in essence dead for several decades, their attitudes are noteworthy. For these once-frozen folks were now thawed, fluid, and overflowing with elation, with ebullience, with unbridled passion, with a love they could not share for so long that was now liberated as if from prison. They were childlike, innocent, and unusually compassionate. They were pleased with little, and thankful for each and every blessed waking moment. In spite of their having lost the best years of their lives, the doctor describes them as "so lacking in bitterness and so richly appreciative of life."

They were "drunk on reality" and "intoxicated with beauty." There was a longing for music, art, nature. Family, friends, the touch of human hands, sex, movement, freedom, *fun*. You know, all of the very best, most basic, most splendid things in this world that most of us foolishly take for granted, as if we could never lose them.

But we could.

The once-immobilized patients were now walking up and down the hallways of the hospital with huge grins plastered all over their formerly blank faces. Lights turned on in eyes where before there were none. Folks who displayed nothing but "an infinite remoteness" for as long as forty-eight years were now engaging each other in fascinating conversations on subjects ranging from the simplest of entities to the most magnificent of them all. Everywhere on the ward, grown men and women were waking up from a long, long sleep to rediscover themselves as if being "born again" in middle age or later. The striking descriptions they give of their "quickening" are telling indeed.

"Look at me, look at me, I can fly like a bird!"

"Wonderful, wonderful! I'm moving inside again ..."

"I feel saved, resurrected, re-born. I feel a sense of health amounting to Grace."

"I feel so good, so full of energy. So tingly, like my blood is champagne."

"I have been hungry and yearning all my life, and now I am full. Appeased. Satisfied. I want nothing more."

"I feel so contented, like I'm at home at last after a long hard journey. Just as warm and peaceful as a cat by the fire."

"If everyone felt as good as I do, nobody would think of quarreling or wars."

"It's a very sweet feeling, very sweet and easy and peaceful. I am grateful to each moment for being itself."

"What a perfect day ... I shall never forget it! It's a joy to be alive on a day like this."

"I've been waiting for L-DOPA for the past 30 years."

"For this it was worth it, my life of disease."

After so much bewildering numbness, at last ethereal bliss. The dramatic and emotional testimonies go on and on, but especially consider this final one: *Heaven is right here down on earth.*

The hospital staff was flabbergasted by the changes that came over the "garden ward" (one worker commented, "All we do is feed and water them") as the drug did its miraculous work and opened eighty doors that had been locked for so many years. Unfortunately, L-DOPA's effect did not last for most of those poor souls, and the vast majority eventually slipped back into their fog, their netherworld, their catatonic trances, nevermore to return to normal consciousness.

However, in spite of this major drawback, there was much to celebrate at Mount Carmel that magical summer of 1969. First of all, the long-suffering patients were finally allowed to emerge from their darkness and once again walk into the light, even if only for a short and blessed while. Secondly, they were able to visit with their beloved families and friends—and vice versa—one more time. And, last but not least, the few who were permanently cured now carried within them a powerful lust for life that never-comatose people rarely come to realize.

Now, ultimately, unavoidably, we arrive at the state of unconsciousness that trumps all others: death. While nobody has ever officially returned from the grave (in the last couple of thousand years anyway) there are enough examples of people who have temporarily crossed over the line to give us a pretty good idea of what awaits us on the other side of the final door. In Dr. Pamela M. Kircher's riveting study of this titillating phenomenon *Love is the Link*, she describes numerous "near-death experiences" (NDEs) among her patients who were clinically dead for several seconds, even minutes, and then came back to life with the most amazing tales to tell. Indeed, the stories they relate and the lessons they learned could inspire the rest of us to truly live rather than merely exist.

People who undergo NDEs typically share several interesting traits. They seem to possess a certain sense of wellness, as if they now realize that everything is all right, and even potentially, eventually, perhaps inevitably perfect. There is a calmness, a wisdom, a serenity to them. They are now endowed with a benevolent spirit, a sympathetic heart, a feeling of being connected to all beings and all things. They oftentimes exhibit extreme sensitivity to violence and other people's pain, even to the point where they cannot bear to watch the news on television. Some report a tremendous increase in psychic powers (ESP, mind reading, precognition, etc.) and there are several cases of "flat-liners" apparently acquiring the ability to heal the sick and crippled through the touch of their hands and the warmth of their compassion.

In general, NDEers become more loving, more responsive, more vital. They now have less interest in material success and more interest in serving others. They often change careers midlife and go into the helping professions. There is a renewed affection for nature, an awareness of a "Oneness," a sense of wonderment at the daily miracles that encircle us if only we open our real eyes and see, truly see them. There is a popular belief among near-death experiencers that everything that happens to them is for a purpose that will ultimately serve their highest good. They are conscious of their lives now having more meaning, more fullness, more satisfaction than ever before. They often speak of the importance of each moment.

They are no longer afraid of dying.

Yes, something remarkable takes place within human beings when they almost go over the edge forever, but instead come back from the very brink. Indeed, some of the individual cases that Dr. Kircher presents in her book are so fantastic as to be almost unbelievable. That is, if they were not absolutely true.

One woman described flying through a tunnel at frightening speed and being attracted to a brilliant white light. As she approached it, she felt herself surrounded by supreme peace and all-encompassing love. It seemed as if she were given the option to remain there in paradise, but she wanted to return to earth to tell her husband about this fabulous place so he wouldn't worry about her. And that is what she did. She died peacefully—oh, so peacefully— two days later.

A number of mothers who almost died while giving birth told of wanting to "stay with the Light," but instead choosing to come back to life because they loved their babies even more than they did Heaven.

One man claimed to have "seen the face of God" while immersed in "pure light."

A middle-aged lady recalled being almost murdered as a toddler during a vicious episode of child abuse. She vividly remembers being "lifted out of her body into a profoundly peaceful place" where God told her she would always be protected by angels. To this day she still feels their comforting presence, especially during times of danger.

A man became convinced as a result of his NDE that "there was no evil," only people who were confused but who would eventually "return to the Great Oneness."

A teenager who barely avoided a horrific high-speed car accident suddenly realized he was "a soul that had existed before this lifetime and that would exist after this body had died." Since his close call, he finds that the "little problems" do not bother him anymore.

One lady who had a serious drinking problem related a particularly effective NDE wherein she met her mother who had died from alcoholism, and this otherworldly conversation inspired her to quit the bottle soon after returning from her vision.

Some people who have lived through unsuccessful suicide attempts come to the realization upon waking in the emergency room that they were put on this planet to learn important lessons, and that killing themselves is no longer an alternative because it is "not in God's plan."

An atheist who tried to commit suicide by slitting her wrists felt her soul leave her body and enter a long tunnel. At first she heard distant bells, then beautiful music, and soon found herself "in the presence of pure Light and Love." After surviving this eye-opening event, she changed her lifestyle from one of self-destructive behavior to a healthier, happier, more spiritual path.

One man recalled seeing everything that had ever happened in his life, especially times when he was extremely unkind to people. In fact, many NDEers describe a "life review" whereby each and every instant is covered, not just the "big ones." They learn that how we treat people in this world is very important. Some even report *feeling how it felt* when they were cruel to others!

A young American soldier who almost perished on a World War II battlefield told of leaving his body and being shown a complete movie of his life. Then he was asked, "What do you have to give?" He didn't know. Next he was asked whether he wanted to return to earth or stay there in the wonderful Light. He decided to come back, mainly because he felt concern for his dear mom, who would be overwhelmed with grief if her son were to die at such an early age. Upon awakening to the tender ministrations of army medics, he had the answer to the first question: LOVE is all we ever have to give.

The author (who herself underwent an NDE at the delicate age of six) concisely sums it up this way: "The main messages of the near-death experience are that the purpose of life is to learn how to be loving to each other and that each moment really does matter."

That is, this present plane of existence is a pretty special time and place. Hopefully we come to comprehend—sooner rather than "later"—just how precious, priceless, and potentially perfect each day, each minute, even every last second is, while we can, while we still possess the God-given ability to do so. Because, you see, not everybody does ...

In the marvelous movie *Awakenings* (loosely based on the book) there is an unforgettable scene where a comatose patient suffering from sleeping sickness wakes up one night from his lengthy slumber. Dr. Sacks (adeptly played by Robin Williams) has been experimenting with L-DOPA in hopes of bringing a man named Leonard (Robert DeNiro in a powerful performance) back to life. He is convinced that just the right dosage will do the trick.

One evening, Leonard is given exactly 1,000 milligrams of the drug before bedtime. After the lights are turned off, the doctor falls asleep in a nearby wheelchair. Upon awaking, he discovers with a start that Leonard's bed is now empty!

As empty as Christ's tomb on Easter morning.

In a near panic, the doctor searches the darkened hospital ward for his apparently mobilized patient. He finds him in the dayroom, sitting in his pajamas at a table beneath a softly glowing lamp. He has pencil and paper in hand and is laboriously scribbling something.

As Dr. Sacks silently approaches, Leonard notices movement and looks up. Upon making his first eye contact with another human being in three decades, there is visible apprehension and even fear displayed on his face. The kindly physician assures him "It's okay," and then asks if he can see what he was writing. Leonard slowly pushes the notepad toward him.

"Leonard" is all it says, in almost unreadable script, as if the author were not used to writing. He points to the name, and with some difficulty pronounces his first word.

"Me."

The good doctor beams brightly from ear to ear, like a young mother seeing her newborn baby for the very first time.

Leonard continues, his vocal chords beginning to loosen after their long hiatus.

"Quiet," he drawls in a raspy, drawn-out voice full of fascination.

Dr. Sacks nods. "It's late," he says gently. "Everyone's asleep."

"Ohhh," he groans, as if the idea of sleep were now repulsive to him.

Then, suddenly, a lightbulb comes on deep within Leonard's eyes. His formerly frozen facial expression gradually changes from one of genuine befuddlement to laser beam intensity, just before he smiles broadly and utters his first sentence in thirty years.

"*I'm* not asleep."

Middle of Night Ode to Joy

It is not death or dying which is tragic,
but rather to have existed without fully participating in life—
that is the deepest personal tragedy.
—Edward Abbey

Middle of night.

I wake up and gaze at the tingling molecules of darkness buzzing around in my bedroom. Something is moving. Something is alive in the room.

Something tells me to go outside. So I get up, grab a coat, and head for the back door.

Walking outside into the semidarkness I feel the cold, fresh night air gather round me. All is quiet. Very quiet. I remember an old Rumi poem, something about "Don't go back to sleep, there are people moving back and forth across the doorsill" in the early morning hours …

I pee in the weeds, listening to the sound of myself "making water" and blessing the earth with it. Returning it. Giving it back.

I look up at the nighttime sky and see that it is clear. Gazing at the stars I spot the Bear, the Big Dipper, the Winter Cross. I peer at the other stars, the nameless stars, the countless millions of stars. They are like pinholes of sacred light in the sky's firmament, like tiny openings, or keyholes, in the blue, blue blackness, like little glimpses of the endless heaven that awaits us just beyond the dark night.

I am not asleep.

And neither is the Universe.

I listen again to the silence. The blessed peace and quiet. And then I hear something. I hear something, with my other ears.

There is something coming. There is something humming.

I sense that there is a very large living creature nearby. Indeed, right next to me. But not an animal. Not exactly.

I listen further, closer. I crouch down on my haunches and stop breathing. There it is. Humming. Humming. Almost like a kitten purring. Or some kind of ethereal music. Then I realize what the noise is.

It is the earth, Mother Earth, softly humming a song, in the middle of the night.

I had heard her before. Years ago, while a young man hitchhiking around North America, I would often find myself waking up in the middle of the night while sleeping outside. I would lay there in my sleeping bag, and slowly wake up, and slowly remember who I was, and where I was. Whether it was a cornfield in South Dakota, or a forest in California, or a railroad siding out in the middle of the desert. Out in the middle of nowhere.

Then I would hear it. Hear her.

Mother Earth humming peacefully. While everyone else was sleeping. Except me. And her. Alone together in "the dead of night." In the life of night.

For the night is not dead. And neither is this planet. She is alive. Very much so. And awake, even at three a.m. And aware. Aware of those who do not sleep in the middle of the night …

I am not asleep.

I look up at the stars again. They are glowing serenely, like many, many little moons, or many, many tiny suns. Like eternal embers of an endless fire, like nocturnal members of an endless tribe, like loving ancestors set in the nighttime sky, just so.

I am not alone.

I hear a faint rustling in the sagebrush. I am not the only one awake. For there are owls, large cats, and other wild animals who do not sleep in middle of night. Those that hunt. Those that search. Those who cannot sleep while there is so much going on.

A bird flies by overhead, high, high above me, but I can hear each flap of its wings, indeed every feather in its flight. I remember a raven I met years ago in the Utah desert. A raven that spoke to me. And told me this:

"Do not do what others do. Do not sleep in middle of night. Do not close your eyes, do not close your ears, do not close your heart to the lessons of night, the lessons of darkness, the teachings of Mother

Earth and Father Sky, the messages from the other world which is not human, the other world that is so much more than human. Do not be normal. Do not be like the others. Listen. Feel. See. Search, and you will find. Find what you are looking for. In the middle of the night."

I stand outside in the darkness, in the darkness that is the true light, the light of night, as long as I can, until the winter chill seeps inside my sparse clothing and I decide to go back into the house.

Just then I hear a coyote's voice off in the distance, off in the southwest. First a yip, then a cry. Then another coyote joins in. Then another. Then full-throated howls as the whole pack, the entire tribe, comes together like a choir and fills the cold night air with the sounds of delirious joy, which is the purest noise of them all, for it is the sound of being alive.

I am chilled to the bone, but it is no longer a cold chill. For every cell in my body is now tingling with ecstasy, with exhilaration, with warmth from a source not of my body's making. I suddenly hear my voice joining in with the coyotes singing. With the Universe singing.

Just singing in the middle of the night, just singing in the middle of nowhere, just singing for dear life. Just singing.

For that is what life is: The sheer living of it, the sheer enjoyment of it, the pure and thus holy exultation in it. To do more than merely exist, to go for the gusto, to accomplish that rarest of all deeds, which is to truly live before you die. That is all, and all-in-all. And that is enough.

That is more than enough.

After a while, the coyotes stop howling their hauntingly beautiful serenade to the sky, and so do I. All is quiet. All is quiet once again. Except for the earth, still softly purring, still softly humming her ancient melody.

A breeze comes up from out of the juniper hills, from out of the sagebrush prairie. I smell wood smoke, and hear a great-horned owl go "hoo, hoo," just twice. I see a falling star. I make a wish. To live well. Real well. Until I die.

I go back inside the house. But not back to bed. For it is a good night.

A good night to be awake.

On the Dark Side of the Earth

What hath night to do with sleep?
—John Milton

Without the contrast of complete opposites, life would be unbearably dull. If not for the cosmic dance of yin and yang, everything would come to a screeching halt. And if there were no alternating schedule of day and night, night and day, we could not tell the difference between darkness and light because all would just be gray. But thankfully there are two distinct sides to each and every coin. This is the story of one of them.

Daytime occurs on this planet whenever one half of its surface is exposed to the intense radiation emanating from the sun. The soothing warmth and invigorating luminescence causes the land to awaken, the creatures to stir, and the vegetation to grow to fruition as if influenced by magic. Even inanimate objects appear to glow from within, sparkle like fish scales, and tingle like living flesh as if they were actually sentient rather than dead. Everything becomes so visible, so obvious, so tangible.

Meanwhile, while one half of the globe is baking in the solar oven, the other one is hiding in the shadows like a great-horned owl. Shielded by its own tremendous mass, the dark side of this world is devoid of the direct rays of the sun and thus able to freely commune with the antithesis of light. As night descends in earnest shortly after dusk, the blackness gathers like a heavy wool blanket and seemingly puts Mother Earth soundly to sleep. However, that is not necessarily the case. For there are certain critters that only come out at night, forms of flora that delight in the darkness, predators that prefer to hunt between sunset and sunrise, and other beings that naturally shy away from the day. For it is much too bright for them.

Because, you see, the shadow this world casts upon itself causes some entities to disappear into the void, while allowing others to flourish like night-blooming primroses. Not all is unilluminated in total darkness, for there is a surreal yet very real source of enlightenment available in the middle of the night due to the relative lack of light. Indeed, the serenity inherent in the hours of darkness enables us to relax, slow down, and enjoy life coming to us, rather than chasing after it like a barking dog as we do during the day. For while the glaring sunshine bombards us with the urgency to do something, to accomplish something, to "make hay when it's sunny," the night instead advises us to mellow out.

Notice how "things change" when the day fades away and is replaced by the clean slate of night. Everything now looks different, peculiar, in fact the exact opposite of normal like a negative photograph that is exposed by darkness rather than by light.

For example, see how the hundreds and thousands of stars gradually become visible even as the closest one disappears like a magician behind a curtain. Likewise, as this side of our planet descends into the dark, the other planets appear in the sky as if they had been hiding all day long in the ether. Watch how Mother Moon rises ever so slowly from behind the earth's horizon like a shy girl unaware of her beauty, beaming with the reflected luminosity of the now-unseen Father Sun. Perceive the coolness, the calmness, the peace and quiet of night after the noise and heat and hustle and bustle of the day.

Feel the effects of darkness on the human body, human mind, human soul. The heart rate decreases, the brain waves flatten out, the spirit is loosened of its earthly bonds and soars like a bald eagle. Notice what the nocturnal phase of this planet does to plants and animals, insects and fish, temperature and weather. Observe the mood swings of nature as it moves from twilight to shadow and back again.

Enjoy the exhilarating aspects of nighttime as well as the restful ones. Feel the spinning motion of this phenomenal world we inhabit, the delirious unstoppable momentum, the spontaneous yet somehow synchronized series of rotations evident in our galaxy. Envision the evolution of the universe from chaos into order, the ever-ongoing attraction of opposing forces, the magnetism and yet the repulsion, the emptiness and yet the fullness, the graceful intercourse of earth and heaven.

Heaven and earth.

Now realize how every single place on this singular planet participates in the daily dance, the nightly waltz, the eternal choreography, the lovely interplay between daylight and darkness, the diurnal and the nocturnal. For when it is sunny in Hawaii, it is pitch black in Mozambique. When it's dawn in New Zealand, it's dusk in France. High noon in Baghdad means midnight in the Yukon. Late in Tokyo is early in Rio. And while morning is warming the east coast of North America, it is cooling off nicely in China.

And vice versa.

Verily, what "goes around" does truly "come around." The celestial cycle continues on and on unabated like a powerful pirouette that can never stop or even decelerate. And for every minute of daylight we are given each year we receive an equal amount of night, liberally adorned and accented by two periods of pearly twilight that occur halfway in between the two exact opposites. This is how perfection works. One thing becomes completely different from the other. One entity is directly, directionally, and diametrically contrasted by another. One side of a revolving wheel heads this way, while the other side goes that way.

In order to understand and thus fully appreciate the lessons of night, our senses must expand beyond the usual five in much the same way the pupils of a cat's eyes enlarge in the dark to allow all available light to enter. For there is so much to partake in on the "other" side of the world that we cannot always visually verify, or audibly hear, or feel with our physical fingertips. Because when our side of the earth is enveloped by the fluffy pillow of night, we cannot always perceive everything that is happening with just our normal faculties. We must use the "extra" ones. We must employ our intuition, our instincts, our imagination, our night vision, our other eyes, our sixth sense, perhaps a seventh one.

Down through the ages, philosophers have proposed the notion that there are as many things invisible to the naked eye as there are those that are observable. Likewise, when darkness descends like a dense fog and hides one half of the globe in its inky embrace, there is still quite a lot of activity going on. It's just not as noticeable as during the day.

Because when something disappears into a place where no light may enter, that does not mean it ceases to exist, any more than something suddenly appearing in the morning did not exist late at night. In other words, an entity that is discernible and then becomes indiscernible is still there, even though we can't always witness it with our supposedly perfect 20/20 vision. And that is the beauty, the wonder, the mystery of life on planet Earth. We cannot see, we cannot know, we cannot comprehend everything. Nor should we.

For the human race is as much fostered by darkness, shadows, and secrecy as it is by daylight, things that are visible, and concepts that are easily understood.

Edge of the Flames

There is an age-old belief that this world, which began in fire, shall also, someday, end in fire. And so, in between these two cataclysmic events, we humans should best enjoy our short and blessed time on this unique and temporary planet. We should experience all of the very finest things in life. Including fire. Especially fire.

While we still can.

Of all the elements, all the entities, all the miracles in existence on earth, there might be none as mysterious, as improbable, as sensational as fire. As warm and soothing, lively and exciting, wild and free. As colorful, as beautiful. As pleasant.

For fire is not only essential for the creation and destruction of this world, it is awfully nice to have around in the meanwhile. Indeed, it is one of those simple pleasures we should all fully partake of before we die. Because fire is not just a comfort, a godsend, and a means to an end. Fire is our companion.

In fact, fire is one of our very oldest friends. For countless eons, we human beings have huddled around its healing flames. Fire has warmed our bodies, kept us dry, cooked our food, provided light for our camps and caves and cabins, soothed our souls during the long winters, hardened our tools, finished our pottery, cauterized our wounds, lit our pipes, brewed our potions, ignited our passions, inflamed our desires, illuminated our ceremonies, and given birth to religion.

Few things are more captivating, more exhilarating, more life-reaffirming than a roaring campfire in the middle of the night. Especially when you are alone. All alone. But you're not.

Are you?

For the spiritual dynamics of this cosmos somehow change late at night, when it is just you and the fire. The two of you. And no one else.

As you tend the fire, as you gently stoke the small but raging inferno, as you stare into the center of the flames, you begin to see

41

things. Real things. And unreal things, also …

There is a tribe in Africa that has developed an interesting coming-of-age test for their young males. It is called "dreaming the fire." In order for a teenage boy to be considered a man, he must stay up all night long, by himself, and stare into the flames of the campfire. If he becomes afraid, he has failed. If he goes inside before morning arrives, he has flunked. If he falls asleep, it doesn't count. For he must witness, without fear, without fright, the very nature of fire, which is nothing less than the meaning of life and death. He must peer deeply into the flames until he is given a vision of what he should do with his precious time on this planet. Then, as dawn comes, he is ready to go hunting with the other men.

Yes, there are fascinating sights to be seen in a campfire late at night. Watch the way the flames play with the wood, the way the flames and the fuel frolic together. It is a union at once fierce yet frail, angry yet happy, earthy yet unearthly. It is destruction, and yet it is creation. Prehistoric yet present, hypnotic yet revealing, peaceful yet cathartic.

Look closely. Go ahead, don't be scared. Soon you will see every color of the rainbow. And not just the oranges and yellows commonly associated with fire, but vivid, splendid, brilliant blues, purples, reds, violets, pinks, and even a rich florescent aquamarine green. Watch the psychedelic light show taking place right in front of your eyes. Witness the ecstatic neon luminosity burning, burning deep within the glowing black embers as they sizzle and shimmer and seem to be breathing in and out, in and out, as if alive.

As night progresses, build log structures in the restless, relentless flames, then watch them slowly disintegrate into ashes. Behold the small explosions that send tiny spaceships sailing off into the nighttime sky. Observe the delicate interaction between darkness and light at their most primal juncture.

Discover the universe, all over again, by firelight. Find that you once again wish to become one with it. For there is something mystical, something ethereal, something almost sacred about fire. The dancing, entrancing, enlightening flames. As if fire were a pure brightness from Heaven itself sent down to earth in the form of lightning to keep us company, to encourage us, to support us, to help us. And even more …

For the essence of fire is perhaps best exemplified by the selfless gracefulness of the flames that light our night even as they disappear into the surrounding darkness, the flames that warm our chilled bodies even as they expire in the cold air, the flames that comfort our souls even as they silently return into the Void from whence they originally came.

At the striking of the first match.

When a man faces his maker, he will have to account for those pleasures of life he failed to experience.
—Talmud

Long before computers and cell phones and video games, television and stereo and radio, electricity and central heating and indoor lighting, there was fire. Fire to entertain us, to keep the blackness away, to heat up our winters, to enliven our minds, to "fire" our imaginations.

Before there were fluorescent lightbulbs, there was fire shining in our primeval eyes, fire gleaming in our ancient souls, fire rising up within our heart of hearts. For long before there was civilization, there was fire.

Blazing like the first desire.

Yes, fire has played a significant role in the history of the human race. And not only for our survival and development, but also our high quality of life down through the ages. And as such, it should not be avoided, but rather enjoyed and appreciated.

Therefore, if you have never spent an entire night "tending the fire," all by yourself, I have a suggestion for you. Do it.

Do it before you die. Find the time, choose the place, take a chance. Savor the golden opportunity to stare into the flames of a campfire, all night long, alone. And see what I mean.

Unless, of course, you are looking forward to that little talk with God, later on, concerning the wonders of this world you somehow failed to experience.

Things That Do Not Fade

There are things in this world that change over time, and there are things that don't. By necessity, the list of the former is quite a bit longer than the latter. Because, you see, almost everything eventually metamorphoses into something else. Sooner or later, practically all entities grow dim and fade away like the glow from a lightbulb in the blackness when it burns out. For it is the basic nature of so very many things to wither, to wane, to dematerialize in the blink of eternity's eye back into the bottomless void from which they initially emanated. Indeed, the list is almost endless.

See how darkness fades into dawn and then into morning, how daylight fades into twilight and then into night. See how the stars dissolve into sky at sunrise, and how sunset dissolves into starlight at dusk. See how the raging bonfire dissipates into embers, the embers into coals, the coals into ashes, the ashes into dust, the dust into the swirling wind. Behold the ringing of a church bell on Sunday morning, the rumble from a freight train crossing the desert, the sound of a siren in the city. Notice how they recede into nothingness as if they had never existed.

Witness the buds of spring, the flowers of summer, the golden leaves of autumn, the blinding-white snowfields of winter. Now witness them disappear. Observe the bloom of the rose, the blush of the tomato, the brilliant green of the grass. The paint on the car, the paint on the house, the paint on the Picasso painting. The color in the T-shirt, the color in the blue jeans, the color in the baseball cap. Watch how they all gradually mutate and ultimately return to the place from whence they came. For it is the essence of most participants in this temporary drama to dwindle, to decline, to diminish, to slowly yet steadily, naturally yet supernaturally, visibly yet invisibly vanish back into the cosmic blender.

Glaciers melt. Lakes evaporate. Streams dry up. Steel turns to rust. Buildings crumble. Towers tumble. Empires collapse. Eras expire. Cultures die. Species become extinct. Things wear out, break down, go kaput, become discarded. The latest electronic gadgets grow old in a matter of months. Even granite tombstones ultimately disintegrate into dust.

So many things that fade like a cheap rug over time. The visions of childhood, the daydreams of adolescence, the nighttime dream that was so impressive this morning but almost forgotten by noon. The ink on a store receipt, the white in a newspaper, the black of brand-new tires. The laughter after a joke, the roar of the crowd following a touchdown, the sound of a radio when you shut it off. The smell of perfume, the fragrance of lilac blossoms, the aroma of freshly baked bread. Campfire smoke, waterfall mist, morning dew. Clouds. Rain. Rainbows. All vaporizing into the air like steam from a kettle on the stove.

Infancy. Innocence. Phases of life. Fads. Fashions. Fascination. Infatuation. First love. Lust. Excitement. Adrenaline. Pleasure. Anger. Hunger. Fullness. Disappointment. Shock. Embarrassment. The longing for vengeance. The enjoyment of arguments. The appetite for competition. The reasons for fighting.

All fading away.

Photographs. Memories. Names. Lessons. Questions. Book covers, batteries, leather boots, favorite toys, lawn furniture. The stink of skunk spray, the stench of a rotting carcass, the scent of a slaughterhouse as you drive past. The pain medication, the alcohol buzz, the magic mushroom trip. Hiccups, headaches, hangovers, sprained ankles, stubbed toes, scraped knuckles, sore muscles, bruises, scars, black eyes, broken hearts.

Notice the ice jam in spring, the water puddle in summer, the aspen forest in fall, the woodpile during winter. The light from a lighthouse the farther you sail out to sea. A coyote howl in the canyon. A symphony of red-winged blackbirds at scarlet dusk. A lonesome train whistle in the middle of the night. All receding like objects in the rearview mirror of a speeding automobile.

The value of money, the worth of possessions, the smell of a new car's interior, the sparkle of the shiny things you buy at the mall that lose half of their luster by the time you get them home. The thrilling commotion of Saturday night on the town as it deteriorates into the dull, numb, blank-faced torpor of Sunday morning coming down. The waxing full moon transforming itself into the waning half moon, then into a slender sliver of a silver crescent at sapphire-splitting dawn, and finally once again back into emptiness.

Chances. Potential. Opportunities. The past. The present. Seconds into minutes into hours into days into weeks into months into years into decades into old age. Hair. Teeth. Sight. Hearing. Health. Your mortal body. Your earthly life. Etcetera.

Yes, there are countless things in this world that are susceptible to time, weather, seasons, growth, culmination, degeneration, and death. The roster goes on and on.

However, of course, there are always two distinctly different sides to every coin, every face, every story. And so it is with the things that fade. For, alternately, ultimately, there are those other entities that do not fade, do not change, do not turn gray and go away. Ever. In fact, in truth, in the divine order, they have no option but to forever remain the same. Naturally, this list is much shorter than the one above.

Real beauty doesn't fade.
—Jurgen Herbst

Now, the very finest gifts in life are also pretty scarce. Because, you see, if this realm were saturated with the exceptional, we would not recognize it as such. We would take the perfect, the heavenly, the undying for granted. And then the rare would not be so special, nor evidence of the sacred so perceivable.

Love. Family. Angels. The soul. The light at the end of the tunnel.

You know. The important stuff.

In essence, the greatest wonders of them all exhibit several similar characteristics. For they take place not only without us, but within us. They are likewise beyond us, and yet of us. They are felt with the heart, rather than the physical senses. And last but not least, they last forever, instead of just a short while.

Therefore, if you want to find out if something is mortal or immortal, ask yourself one simple question. Does it fade? Because the things that fade away over time are from this temporary side of existence, while the entities that do not are from the other, timeless, eternal one.

Angel in the Room

Three out of four Americans believe in angels.
—ABC News, 2011

Some events are not supposed to be forgotten. For there are experiences in this world that are so striking, so profound, so bubble-bursting remarkable they are meant to be remembered. Even if they cannot be explained, rationalized, or proven by modern science, these vivid memories should not be disregarded or swept underneath the rug. Because oftentimes the most real things of this realm are the ones we cannot visually see, audibly hear, or actually reach out and touch, yet we know that they exist because we feel them not with our senses but rather with our heart. So it is with angels.

The genesis for this story came in the middle of a cold winter's night when the wind chill outside was forty degrees below zero, and yet there was a warmth in my bedroom that no furnace could produce. As I scribbled down the ideas rushing into my head at 3 a.m. in a half-awake, half-still-dreaming state, there was a presence of friendly spirits in the house as real as the pen and paper in my hands. It reminded me of when I was a child and had playmates only I could see, the kind that would play with me in the backyard when I was "all alone."

But I wasn't.

For it seems that I was provided with an invisible partner at birth, or perhaps several of them, and he/she/they have been a constant source of joy, friendship, sound advice, silent warnings, and gentle nudges throughout my entire life. However, as I neared maturity the adults warned me to give up these "imaginary beings" because they were not real and therefore would do me no good. How wrong they were.

Over the years I became quite fond of "the other side of reality," which is the stuff that normal grownups never acknowledge because they are too busy with the minutiae of this side. Indeed, by the time I was a teenager I realized there were more things that are not obvious or visible or verifiable than there were things that are. I discovered that the sights seen out of the corner of my eye, while disappearing before I could look at them, were nonetheless more genuine to me than any human counsel to the contrary. Rather than being distracting or disturbing, these images became my comfort and companion.

Years ago I met a medicine woman in Colorado and we became fast friends. Several months later she told me, "I liked you right away because I could tell that you had never abandoned your muse." Not familiar with the word, I inquired as to its meaning. She explained that a muse is a special connection to God which is given to each soul at conception, and as we grow from babies to adolescents to adults we choose whether to remain attached or not. This celestial yet earthly being is referred to as "guardian angel" by Catholics, "spirit guide" by Native Americans, "messenger" by the early Greeks, "the Other" by German philosophers, "source of inspiration" by poets, and "first helper" by me.

Over the course of my lifetime I have stayed in touch with this thing, this essence, this whisper in my ear, this ethereal advisor, this outrageous angel of mine. And vice versa. For I learned early on to trust my instincts, my "hunches," my unexplainable and almost involuntary decisions to occasionally do the exact opposite of the logical. Because, you see, they work.

The premise I am proposing—that angels are real, and not some hallucination, religious creation, or medieval fantasy—may not be convincing to all who read these words, for not everyone has experienced what I have. But know this: There is more going on in this life, in this world, and in this universe than meets the mortal eye.

Allow me to share a few examples of precisely what I mean.

At age sixteen I had a summer job working for the city parks department. One day a buddy and I were riding on the tailgate of a pickup truck as the man at the wheel drove like a maniac through Pawnee Park. Suddenly we hit a big bump and my body went airborne. Just before hitting the ground I distinctly heard a familiar voice say "Roll." And roll I did. Instantly imagining myself as a rotating ball instead of flailing arms and legs, I eventually came to rest in a bush by the side of the road. Rather than breaking bones or cracking my head wide open on the gravel surface, all I had to show for my improvised acrobatics was a small scrape on one elbow.

One time during my "experimental years" I got ahold of some poisonous psilocybin mushrooms and took off on the bad trip of all bad trips. Indeed, I found myself floating from one horrible level of hell to even more horrible levels of hell, one right after another. Then, as I was curled up on the floor in the fetal position rocking back and forth, a small gray and white kitten entered the room. She immediately came over and laid her body on top of mine, gently kneading me with her claws and purring like a Sherman tank. In the midst of severe psychic peril, I somehow knew that this animal was my unlikely yet only connection to sanity. And so, little by little, I rode out the worst ride of my life and gradually made it back home to reality with the help of my tiny friend.

Later on, I asked my roommates where the magical cat had come from. Nobody else had seen her.

After my grandfather was struck and killed by a passenger train, they printed a photograph of his body, covered by a white sheet, on the front page of the local newspaper. Upon witnessing the pure white spot in the somber gray picture, I clearly remember seeing an angel's face there, for only a split second, but with just that one quick look she told me not to worry about Grandpa anymore, for "He's with us now."

Shortly after learning of my brother Bruce's untimely death by avalanche at age twenty-nine, I found myself alone in my apartment late at night, crying out loud. Then, as the wails were escaping from my very soul, I heard other voices in the room, weeping with me. Dozens of them, perhaps a hundred or more. For a whole host of heavenly spirits had come to commiserate in my hour of need. And no, they were not crying for my brother, who was now in a better place. They were crying for me, and with me, because they were the only ones who could comfort me during my longest night.

A few days later I related this astonishing incident to Bruce's longtime girlfriend Rhonda. During my story, her eyes grew steadily larger and larger until she finally exclaimed, "The same thing happened to me!"

For she too had heard the angels.

While taking care of my father during the final four months of his life, there were occasions when I was required to do things that I had no knowledge of, experience with, or stomach for. And yet they were done. How? Call it imagination if you like, or divine intervention if you will, or an out-of-body episode if you know what I mean, but I would sometimes find myself *watching myself* perform delicate procedures as if someone else were taking over for me when my energy or understanding or compassion ran out.

Like an invisible nurse come to the rescue.

While some will no doubt deem these extraordinary occurrences to be impossible, they are nevertheless true. For again, there is more—oh, so much more—that the human mind cannot comprehend than it can.

Perhaps people who do not believe in angels need to once again open their minds to the other side of life as they did when they were children. Because there is a place—in fact, right down here on earth—where heavenly beings are still available, still reachable, still willing and able to help us make it through this strange, troubling, often painful existence.

If only we acknowledge the messengers.

Pay attention to these silent voices, these unseeable hands, these unseen visitations from beyond the veil that only partially separates life from death. Because our angels are not here to bother or frighten, but rather to assist and enlighten. Simply put, they just want us to be happy.

A few questions before closing:

What was with you when you were born? What is with you late at night when you cannot sleep? What gives you the strength to go on when you have none left? What pushes you out of harm's way at the last second? What makes you smile not long after you have cried? What puts the twinkle back in your eye after you thought it was gone forever? What provides you with such pleasant company even when you are "all alone?"

Who will be there when you die?

For there is one thing we all possess that will not pass away when we do. There is one true friend who will never abandon us, no matter how old, crippled, or decrepit we may become. There is one relationship that is always salvageable no matter how long we may have ignored it. And there is one headlight shining perpetually in the darkness to guide us on our journey home.

If only we turn it on.

One more thing. The whole while I was lying in bed in the middle of the night writing down notes for this article, my cat sat stock-still on my stomach, staring wide-eyed past my right shoulder as if there were somebody else present in the room.

The Mother Goddess Mountain

She's up there.

Although I cannot see her, I know that she is there. Lying peacefully on her back, at 13,000 feet, in the middle of the LaPlata Mountains, in the middle of the night, in the middle of the raging blizzard. In the very center of the universe. For all roads, all streets, all paths, all animal trails lead to Squaw Mountain. My home on earth. Even when I am not there.

I was introduced to Squaw Mountain by a crusty old miner in the spring of 1975. My buddy Steve and I were hiking around in lower LaPlata Canyon on a fine sunny "bluebird day" when we looked up and saw it. Saw *her*. A huge, wide, almost-vertical, south-facing wall of white snow and gray granite rising steeply, majestically, almost impossibly out of the V-shaped canyon. It appeared to me like something from out of a dream, or vision, or ancient memory.

It reminded me of an old black-and-white photograph I had once seen of Mount Everest. Looming high above all the rest of the mountains, it looked like Valhalla, like Shangri-la, like the throne of the Frost Giants. It looked like Heaven itself to me.

I asked my friend, "What's the name of that mountain?" but he didn't know.

Later, we were trudging through the snow somewhere northwest of Mayday when we came upon an old man. He was wearing tattered brown coveralls, huge snowshoes, and a baseball cap. Introducing himself as "Hawkens," he welcomed us to his neighborhood.

Now, although Steve and I were just a couple of eighteen-year-old punks, he seemed to take an interest in our interest in the mountains, and invited us to his cabin. There we met his lovely wife and drank hot chocolate out of well-worn mugs. The walls of the square one-room shack were covered with drawings and photos of wild mountains and wild animals and wild people. Hawkens was seventy-three years young at the time, with a genuine gleam in his eye and a perpetual half-grin on his tanned, grizzly, untamed face.

He had been mining these "hills" for silver, gold, and fluoride since 1927, mostly by himself.

"Never got rich at it," he proclaimed with a gap-toothed smile, "but then me and Ma never needed a whole lot to be happy anyways."

When it was time to go, Steve and I said our thanks to "Ma," and left her blushing like a goddess in the kitchen. We walked outside into the brilliant sunshine with Hawkens, and I got the feeling that he was most at home when he was outdoors.

Just before leaving, I remembered something. Looking to the north, I asked Hawkens, "What is the name of that mountain?"

His weathered old countenance suddenly lit up with a light from a source not merely human.

"That one there? Why, that's my girl! Her name is Squaw Mountain." With a wink and a hearty chuckle he added, "She's been here longer than me."

Hawkens pointed to the top ridgeline, a long bumpy crest running east and west four thousand feet above us. With an outrageous twinkle in his eye, he showed us the silhouette of an Indian woman lying on her back. The outline of her face, etched against the blue sky, the feather sticking up out of the top of her head, the neck, the breasts, the flat horizontal belly, the swelling hips, the long legs, even her feet. Which appeared to be wearing moccasins.

A light clicked on in my eyes, or in my head, or perhaps in my heart. Something was communicating with me. Something ethereal. Yet real. My young vision instantly opened up another notch, and I saw a side of nature not seen before in this lifetime. For I now recognized in this mountain not only the sheer beauty of Mother Earth, but suddenly the human element in nature, and beyond that, the natural element, or natural blessings, bestowed upon us humans. Indeed, inherent within us, if only we look.

The mountain gods were smiling down on me that day. Sharing a secret. Telling me an old story.

Back in early Greece, and over in China, and even here in North America there are what are called "Mother Goddess mountains." Now, while this term can be rightly applied to a gently rounded hill, or a peak with two summits, it is perhaps best bestowed upon a set of three mountains, placed ... just ... so.

Basically, there are two similar, or "twin," peaks (female breasts) framing a round mountain in between (the belly). Ancient religions often built their temples and shrines in the perfect location to view this soothing scenario, which is nothing less than the appearance of Mother Earth, on her back, giving birth, before our eyes. Giving birth to us.

Twenty years after my initial experience with Squaw Mountain, I was living up in Silverton when I met a medicine woman. Yes, a medicine woman. Indeed, she once cured a bad case of poison oak I had gotten in Utah with a slice of tofu. She is the one who first told me about Mother Goddess mountains, and I have been seeing them everywhere in southwestern Colorado ever since.

And I find it to be an incredible coincidence—yet not really a shock—that the "face" of Squaw Mountain reminds me of the medicine woman's profile.

It is now ten years later, and I live on a piece of land twelve miles due south of Squaw Mountain. From my backyard she sets far up in LaPlata Canyon, six thousand feet above me, facing the sun, framed perfectly by Parrot Peak on the left and Deadwood Mountain on the right, and surrounded by other holy summits with names like Silver, Lavender, and Hesperus. Squaw Mountain has become a daily joy to me, and a constant source of inspiration, and I have never seen her look the same way twice.

I should explain that you won't likely find "Squaw Mountain" listed on any map of this area. Indeed, it is only the old-timers who call it by that name, for the 1963 USGS topographical quad does not even identify this massive massif except to list its westernmost summit as "Spiller Peak" (13,123') and its easternmost summit as "Babcock Peak" (13,149'). So most of the younger crowd call it Spiller, or Babcock, or "the Knife Ridge." But it is not.

It is Squaw Mountain. Why? Because it looks like a woman lying on her back. On top of a mountain.

But not always. From different angles this magical peak sometimes appears to be other things. From Tomahawk Basin it looks like a pair of horns on a bull elk. From Neptune Gulch it seems to be a mighty hawk spreading its wings and rising into the air. And from Boren Creek, below the enormous south face, it reminds me of a wolf.

But one thing is certain. The mountain is always beautiful. And she always will be. Even when hidden by clouds, even when hidden by other mountains. Even in the midst of a raging midwinter snowstorm, she is beautiful.

For she is the Gray Princess. The Rock Maiden. The Lady in Stone. The lovely Indian woman, lying on her lofty bed at the crest of the LaPlata Mountains, so peaceful and relaxed. Sometimes asleep. Sometimes awake. Sometimes staring up at the sky. The deep, rich, neon-cerulean-blue Colorado sky.

Other times she entices the clouds, the gray and white clouds, to come and touch her, to lie down low on her like a blanket. A gray and white woolen blanket with designs spawned out in the desert and spun upon special looms above timberline. Gray and black and white, but also turquoise, canary, and maroon. Colors from ancient canyons and enchanted forests. Colors like the ones I saw in the womb, the ones I see behind closed eyelids, and the ones that I will see beyond the grave. Colors of day, and colors of night, and colors of twilight, passing each other in the sky.

Colors like the surreal green glow I sometimes see in the sunrises and sunsets of this sacred land.

Colors of heaven … on earth.

For that is what Squaw Mountain is to me now: a tangible piece of heaven, right here on earth. The Goddess Incarnate, if you will.

And yet, she is just an ethereal wisp of a veil of a memory of a vision of some place I have been to before, in some spiritual realm far beyond this earth and this life and this sky.

A place, a high place, a holy place, a holy mountain. The Mother Goddess Mountain.

Up there in the clouds.

The Upper Falls

The first time I met Dolores, all she said to me was "Ugh."

Having recently moved to Silverton, Colorado, I was busy working on my first book while living in an old barn and doing odd jobs for the landlord. Since there was no door-to-door mail delivery in town, everybody had a box at the downtown post office and would pick up their letters and packages on a daily or weekly or, in some cases, monthly basis. Naturally, the gray building on the corner became one of the main meeting places in San Juan County (along with the Miner's Tavern and Gold King Café) and people would often stop there as much for the conversation and latest gossip as to check their mailboxes.

Not long after arriving, someone told me that Dolores LaChapelle, the renowned skier, climber, author, and visionary was living in Silverton. What an amazing coincidence! Of course, I began looking forward to the possibility of someday actually meeting her.

One winter morning while walking up the stairs to the post office, I noticed an old woman on the inside slowly hobbling my way. Quickening my footsteps I reached the front door shortly before she did and held it open for her. As she shuffled past in obvious agony, all she could do was grunt her thanks to me for my small favor, and then carefully make her way to her car. Watching in silent awe, I said to myself, "Wow, that was Dolores LaChapelle."

Years earlier I had been introduced to her writings while living in Salt Lake City, and *Earth Wisdom* is still one of the very few books that honestly changed my life. While having already discovered the earthly yet heavenly delights of climbing mountains, skiing deep powder, and exploring the wildest places in North America, her vivid descriptions, reverent philosophy, and instinctual communication with nature only served to confirm and verify what I had begun to learn on my own. My cherished copy of her classic became so well worn after being passed around among friends that it began coming apart at the binding. Little did I know at the time that years later the author herself would hand me a mint condition copy (so rare as to be priceless) to replace the one that was literally falling to pieces.

The second time I ran into Dolores at the post office came several months after the first. She was moving much better now, and the previous grimace of pain on her face was supplanted by a glowing light. Come to find out, she had undergone extensive surgery on both hips to repair the damage done by a long-ago avalanche, and the recuperation period was not easy, even for her.

Approaching the living legend with the silver braided hair as she was about to get into her car, I felt a sudden surge of nervousness in my belly, which is unusual for a big galut like me.

"Excuse me," I said, "are you Dolores LaChapelle?"

She looked me straight in the eye. "Yes. Who are you?"

After telling her my name, and mentioning that I lived over on Mineral Street, she curtly inquired, "What are you doing here?" (at a small former mining town in the middle of the San Juan Mountains).

"I'm writing a book," I replied.

Her eyes became curious. "Oh. What about?"

"Hitchhiking and skid row and high mountains."

"Oh, like Jack Kerouac," she smiled.

"Exactly!"

We hit it off right away. I explained how her books had shed a bright light on my life's path, and we opened up to each other surprisingly easy. I had often heard how famous people, especially writers, are usually a big disappointment when you meet them because they are so in love with themselves that their egos take over. However, Dolores could not have been more the opposite. Indeed, she was one of the most sincere, delightful, and pleasant people I ever had the pleasure of meeting.

The first time I visited her cabin she made me feel instantly at home. As we chatted in the sunroom just off of her kitchen, I couldn't help but notice how much she reminded me of my dear departed Grandma out on the farm and how we used to sit in her sunny kitchen and talk about anything and everything that came into our heads.

Later that afternoon while leaving Dolores's place, I felt like I had just guzzled a bottle of champagne instead of sipping on the cup of tea she offered me after lunch.

Over the next few months and years we became good friends, and I thanked my lucky stars each and every time I saw her. I helped her with her firewood, and she helped me with my writing.

What was especially curious was the wide variety of opinions the folks in Silverton expressed about their illustrious neighbor. A number of people openly gushed while sharing stories of how decent and warm and loving Dolores was. How considerate, how concerned, how kindhearted. How she had taught their children to ski, showed the adults how to do Tai Chi, and helped old Lorenzo beat cancer, all of it for free. How she guided her pupils to see the beauty and wonder and magic of this world, to "live between heaven and earth."

And yet there were other locals who confided in me that Dolores was cold and creepy. One man even described her as a "mean old witch." She was stuck up. She was strange. She did weird things, wrote weird books, had weird friends.

Apparently the slender old lady with the lyrical name and larger-than-life persona was either an angel incarnate or the devil herself, depending on who you talked to.

The truth of the matter, deciphered over time, was that Dolores had great patience with anyone who was real, honest, and striving to live well, but none whatsoever for the others. Simply put, the phonies of this world despised Dolores with a passion.

While the rest of us loved her even more.

Mary Dolores Greenwell was born on Independence Day, 1924, in Louisville, Kentucky. While growing up in Denver, she developed an early love of the Rocky Mountains. During the war years she and her sister would hitchhike to the high country on camping and climbing trips. While still a teenager, she and two friends made the first ascent of Scepter Peak in the Needles Range of southwest Colorado. Just before descending, Dolores wrote their names on a piece of paper and left it there inside of an empty lipstick container.

Imagine the looks on the faces of the famous Swiss mountaineers who climbed this towering pinnacle years later, thinking they were the very first, only to discover a lipstick case on the summit!

Shortly after finishing college, Dolores moved west to Aspen. Not long after learning to ski, she got a job teaching others how to do it. During a climbing trip to the Canadian Rockies, she met

Ed LaChapelle. Together they traveled the globe doing important research on glaciers, avalanches, and the mysterious physics of snow. They eventually settled in Alta, Utah, where Dolores became known as the "Best Woman Powder Skier in the World." She also earned the title "Witch of the Wasatch" for her uncanny ability to predict storms, snow conditions, and when the blue columbines would bloom.

Twenty years later they moved to Silverton, where she wrote her third book, the masterpiece *Earth Wisdom*.

Although she authored seven wonder-full books on subjects ranging from Tai Chi, powder skiing and sacred sex to seasonal festivals, D. H. Lawrence and Deep Ecology, Dolores nonetheless insisted that she was merely an "information dispenser" rather than a talented wordsmith. People came from all over the world to consult with her, and she was in constant demand to appear at conferences and workshops, a practice she gave up in later years so she could spend more time "walking the beautiful trail" (as the Navajos put it).

One fine summer day in 1996, Dolores suggested that we "go and see the waterfalls." Not far from town was a huge glacier-carved canyon with a series of cascades on a rushing, gushing, spring-fed stream. Over the years this enchanted spot had become a favorite picnic site for natives and tourists alike. However, most folks would just visit the lower waterfall, pretty as it is, without ever venturing higher to witness the other ones.

The upper ones.

Although still recovering from hip surgery, Dolores led the way up the faint path on the right side of the softly roaring creek. Using her trusty well-worn three-foot ice axe for support, she moved slowly but gracefully along the edge of the steep cliffs, stopping here and there to point out things to her thoroughly mesmerized student.

Due to the constant mist and abundant moisture from the half dozen cataracts, a unique ecosystem has developed here like a rain forest that more resembles the North Cascades than southern Colorado. There's moss and lichen almost everywhere, including a pure white species I had never seen before. There are a number of exotic plants not common to this area, including balsam firs, enormous ferns, and Fairyslipper orchids. At one point near the middle of the upper falls is a sturdy log dam built by Austrian miners a hundred years ago. Beneath it is formed the prettiest pool of water my eyes have ever witnessed. With a childlike grin on her chipmunk face, Dolores told me that this magical pond is known as "Sensuous Serene." Indeed, the photograph I have of the pool and surrounding rocks, while not doing it justice, yet glitters like orange and jade jewels in my hand.

When we reached the top, we cut over to the jeep road and strolled back down to the truck. Years later I learned that the people Dolores took to this secret, sacred, energizing place were those "who needed it."

Indeed, her message to me that day seemed to be, "Look past the obvious. See beyond the book cover, the smiley face, the surface of things. Do not settle for the mundane when you have access to the marvelous. Go further, climb higher, be wilder. Most people only visit the lower waterfalls."

Dolores taught me to find the upper ones.

There is a mysterious interconnection between the physical actions and the state of consciousness one desires.
—From *Earth Wisdom*

During her long and fruitful life, Dolores LaChapelle accomplished many things, and yet on the day before she died she declared, "I did nothing." Rather than listing her numerous achievements and honors, perhaps it would better serve the reader to focus on other aspects of her being. For one thing, Dolores loved to ski. Whether fast on the hardpack, or slower in the powder, she loved motion and rhythm and timing. She loved the freedom, the unfettered movement, the blissful feeling of flight as one descends the mountain in perfect harmony with millions of sparkling snowflakes. She lived for this essence, this unrivaled elegance, this divine dance with gravity and space, the balance and grace, the complete communion with Mother Nature, the privilege of "being so well played."

Powder snow skiing is not fun.
It's life, fully lived, life lived in a blaze *of reality.*
What we experience in powder is the original human self,
which lies deeply inside each of us, still undamaged in spite of
what our present culture tries to do to us. Once experienced,
this kind of living is recognized as the only way to live—
fully aware of the earth and the sky and the gods and you,
the mortal, playing among them.

—From *Deep Powder Snow*

Dolores had a smile like an earthly moon goddess, eyes like twin twinkling stars, and a laugh just like a little girl. Her favorite word was "outrageous," and when she said the middle syllable her voice would deepen and warble like a cross between a grizzly bear and a meadowlark.

Although well educated, extremely intelligent, and quite famous, Dolores was yet one of the most down-to-earth, accessible, and generous people I have ever met. In fact, she spent a large part of her blessed time on this planet showing other less-evolved souls what to do, where to go, and how to be happy through the gentle force of her good nature, natural warmth, and simple charm. There aren't many like that.

More than a friend, she seemed like a family member to me, or beloved elder of the tribe who had taken me under her wing. She shared secrets about wild things, wildflowers, wild animals, wild people, and how to move through this still-wild, still-untamed, miracle-saturated world.

For, you see, Dolores was a teacher. A real one. Her tremendous interest in everything and insatiable appetite for knowledge led her to acquire so much wisdom that she could not help but give it away to others. Her understanding of the human body, study of plants and potions, and research of both Native American and Oriental medicine was quite impressive to say the least.

Like all extraordinary souls, there was more than one side to Dolores. For instance, she could be as ornery and obstinate as a Missouri mule, and yet as caring and compassionate as Mother Teresa. Her gifted son David wrote about "the fierce fire of her willpower," and I have never known anybody who could burn so white-hot when angry, and yet beam so brightly when "tickled pink," which she often was.

In closing, I would like to relate a small incident that will hopefully reveal a tiny facet of this most remarkable diamond to anyone who did not have the good fortune to meet Dolores in person before she left this plane of existence for even higher mountains.

While living in Silverton I subscribed to a backcountry ski magazine named *Couloir*. One day after picking up the new issue at the post office, I stopped by Dolores's house and lent her the copy without even looking at it. She casually opened it and discovered there was a feature story about her inside, complete with color photographs! She just smiled and said, "Oh, that crazy lady who interviewed me a while back ... ," and then laid the magazine down on her desk as if it were no big deal.

We talked for a bit, and then I left. Reaching my truck, I remembered something I meant to tell Dolores, so I walked back through the front door, fully expecting to find her reading the article. Instead, she was in the kitchen. "I'm in here," she called out. Rounding the corner, I saw that she was busy at the sink. "What are you doing?" I asked. She was scrubbing on her old blue and brown daypack with a soapy brush. "Oh, I'm trying to get this oil stain out," she replied.

Imagine. Instead of voraciously perusing the piece about herself in a national magazine—as 99 percent of us would—she was putting things in their proper perspective, and therefore cleaning her pack first.

For Dolores had her priorities straight.

Everything is interconnected ... the real self is part of the whole and thus does not end with death.
—From *Earth Wisdom*

On January 21, 2007, Dolores Greenwell LaChapelle passed away at the age of eighty-two in her sunny, cheerful, cozy cabin at the north end of Baker's Park. I had called her on the phone one month earlier, on the Winter Solstice as I always did, and we talked for a short while. Then there was a visitor at the door, and she wished me well before we said goodbye.

Adios, Mountain Mama.

Now I do not know what happens to us after we die, for that is the ultimate mystery of them all, one which I have yet to experience. But I do take comfort in believing that wherever she is, Dolores is once again dancing in the deep and steep with a great big smile on her face, a little girl giggle in her voice, and a healthy new pair of indestructible hips.

Snow Light

The brightness of the snow
Fills the house with calm.
—Santōka Taneda

Have you ever read a book by candlelight? Have you ever cooked supper by firelight? Have you ever walked home late at night in the silvery luster of a full moon? Have you ever watched a herd of wild animals beneath a starlit sky? Have you ever seen your lover's eyes gleam in the pure glow of a freshly fallen snow?

If not, you should try it some time. For the very best things in life are not always visible under artificial light.

One winter up in Silverton, Colorado (elevation 9,300 feet), we had a two-week-long snowstorm. And I do mean long. This outrageous, mythical, now legendary blizzard straight from hell—shortly after it froze over—began on the first day of February and did not stop until the afternoon of the fourteenth. It dumped so much powder in the San Juan Mountains that even I, a seasoned backcountry skier, was sick of the white stuff.

Well, maybe slightly nauseated.

My girlfriend and I were living in a remodeled horse barn at the south end of town. This was where the wind came howling out of the Animas River canyon like a pack of ferocious wolves, carrying with them a steady supply of fresh snow. And so, every morning for two solid weeks, I would venture outside into the raging storm with my trusty Grain Hog snow shovel. That is, if I could get out the front door. One time, I had to actually exit the house via the kitchen window. Why the kitchen window, you might ask? Because that's the only one that was not completely clogged with snow.

Each day I would clean off the front porch, clear the window wells, and shovel the walkway to the road. Then I would spend the next couple of hours digging out Judith's car and my pickup truck from the wind-packed powder. Excellent exercise, of course, but not exactly enjoyable, especially when the snow is still "falling sideways" in flakes the size of silver dollars.

Then, each and every bleeping night, no matter where I parked them, both vehicles would vanish back into the white void, disappearing underneath a snowdrift roughly the size of a two-car garage.

Finally, one fine afternoon in the middle of February, the wind died, the storm broke, the clouds lifted, and we were treated to quite a sight. For the entire valley, the whole Baker's Park sugar bowl, every last bit of it, had turned utterly, totally, majestically, immaculately white. Room-brightening, eye-dazzling, mind-blowing, get-your-butt-outside WHITE. Indeed, a shade of white that was, as they say, "pure as the driven snow."

That evening Judith and I walked downtown for Valentine's Day supper, enveloped in the surreal glow of six feet of recent snow that had been piled and plowed into miniature mountain ranges in the middle of the streets (since there was no place else to put it). Then, later on, as we were headed back for home in the stunning stillness and absolute silence of the Colorado high country after a big dump, the power went out.

Poof.

Every electric light in Silverton was suddenly blank, and we found ourselves instantly surrounded instead by a different sort of light, one that was definitely not of human origin. For there was an eerie yet soothing luminescence everywhere now, a silky-smooth presence in the night, a mystical aura like never before. Even without streetlights or porch lights or lighted windows in houses, even without starlight, we easily found our way just by using the light of the snow, emanating from below, to see by. It was as if this wonderful white stuff was not just frozen ice crystals, but rather closely related to sun and moon and sky, and had literally fallen to earth from the heavens to illuminate our path.

Indeed, the empty streets were so quiet, so enchanted, so profoundly well lit we wound up taking "the long way home." For we were now like two little kids on Christmas eve, with no grownups around, and therefore could do anything we wanted to in the snow light that was so bright, so brilliant, so radiant we could see its reflection off the clouds overhead.

Snow light, snow bright, won't you light my town tonight.

Later that evening, when the power came back on, we were both startled and disappointed as the artificial lights and electrical noises once again invaded our pristine snow castle of earthly delights and celestial pleasures.

Yes, fresh snow is awesome stuff. And if you have ever spent a winter in the Rockies, survived a two-week blizzard, or skied "champagne powder" (very dry snow with a moisture content of less than 5 percent) you surely know what I mean. It is also pretty scarce. Sometimes while skiing the backcountry I wonder if snow falls anywhere else in the entire universe other than here on this unique and precious little planet. I doubt it. For that would require all of the thousand and one perfect conditions that possibly only exist here on Earth. And so we human beings, or at least those of us who enjoy playing in the snow, are mighty lucky souls. Because, you see, this substance, this essence, this ecstasy incarnate we call "snow" is a magical thing. And, much like real magic, it is difficult to describe, or explain, for there are not many words that work. Just a few.

I have heard that Eskimos in the Arctic use twenty-five different names for snow, while people who live in tropical regions possess no word at all for the frozen white precipitation that they, of course, have never encountered. We Americans lie somewhere in between these two extremes. Actually, though, other than skier phrases such as powder, sugar, graupel, wallboard, windcrust, Sierra cement, mashed potatoes, death cookies, and cream corn, there are very few English terms for snow other than "slush" (wet snow), and "fluff" (dry snow), and well, that's about it. It's as if this short, simple, one-syllable appellation "snow" effectively describes the miraculous stuff that falls from the sky during the winter months. And what a fine word it is …

Now, the term itself is descended from the Anglo-Saxon "snaw," and further back the Indo-European "snoigwhos." It is related to the German "schnee," Russian "snieg," Old Irish "snechta," and the Viking word "skidh," which means to "slide on snow."

And that's the great thing about snow. Not only is it easy on the eyes, but you can have so much fun with it. You can slide on it. You can sled on it. You can ski on it. You can snowboard, windsurf, and even ice skate on it after it melts and then refreezes rock solid.

You can build a snowman with it, a snow fort, an igloo. You can throw snowballs, make snow angels, and roll around in it after soaking in hot springs. You can put it in your cooler to keep the beer nice and cold. You can eat it, or melt it into pure drinking water, or use it to douse a campfire. You can examine the flakes underneath a microscope and observe the divinely inspired one-of-a-kind designs that are exposed there. You can go for a walk around the neighborhood after a storm and check out all the lovely patterns that the wind has carved the snow into. And you can open all the window shades in your house and let the snow light up every room like there were fluorescent lightbulbs hidden inside the walls.

One of my favorite annual events has always been the first snowfall of winter, especially if it comes during the night. What a marvelous, almost supernatural experience it is when you go to sleep in one world and wake up in quite yet another. For even during—especially during—the total darkness, the holy manna from heaven has lit the entire landscape like a giant lamp, like a million nightlights plugged in everywhere, like an old Walt Disney movie, like a full moon illuminating everything in its velvet, creamy embrace.

Indeed, snow often reminds me of the moon, in several ways, for both are white, and bright, and glowing serenely even in the midst of the blackest night. Neither one will ever absorb light, but rather selflessly reflect it, so all may see.

Yes, snow literally shines in the darkness, and I am fascinated by the fact that it falls during the dreariest, bleakest, coldest time of year, when the days are the shortest and the nights the longest, thus giving us this ethereal yet tangible thing, this blessed comfort, this hope, this light, just when we need it the most.

Therefore, the next time it snows, be sure to go for a walk on the new white carpet. Savor the rare tranquility of the scenery that appears, as if by magic, only during this wondrous season of winter. Give your eyes a treat, a Christmas present, a break from being inside all the time. Get outdoors and witness the world adorned in its finest raiment, as the blackness and brownness and grayness of ordinary existence is now covered with white. Pure, fresh, beaming, sparkling, pearly-gates-of-heaven white.

In other words, that splendidly perfect, colorless color that so many people, and so many planets, never get to experience, behold, or relish like we do.

Yes, take a good look at the brilliant white glow that is produced by the brand-new snow now lying on the ground, covering the houses, hiding the cars, and hanging from every bush and tree branch and fenceline, for this is truly one of the prettiest sights you will ever witness.

Because there is no light, anywhere else in the known universe, quite like snow light.

Window Full of Rain

I see first lots of things which dance ... then
everything becomes gradually connected.
—Jim Morrison

I made it all the way to third grade before they finally figured out
I was half blind. You see, I began to realize at an early age that
there was "something wrong" with my eyes, or at least abnormal, or
perhaps just different, but I did not want this to be discovered by the
grownups for fear they would force me to wear spectacles and look
like a bookworm.

So I learned ways of compensating by utilizing my other senses
more, thereby staying one step ahead of the game. I developed little
tricks to keep the secret all to myself. For instance, when the school
nurse came by St. Bon's once a year to check our eyesight, I would
make sure to be one of the last kids examined. While standing in
line, I would memorize what the other children ahead of me recited
as the lady in white pointed to the blurry letters on the eyechart. And
these methods worked fine, at least for the first few years. Then,
come Sister Claudia's class, they caught me.

Of course, I was promptly sent to an eye doctor for further
testing, and there was no way possible to outsmart their machines,
light beams, and revolving charts. They had me dead to rights.

And so came the fateful trip to Omaha with my father to pick up
my new eyeglasses. I still recall the first time I put them on. Sitting
there in the doctor's office, suddenly everything "came into focus,"
literally in the blink of an eye. Not only the nearby things that I
could always make out, but also objects from across the room, and
outside the window, and even the clouds up in the sky, which I had
never really seen before.

On the ninety-mile drive back to town I found myself
mesmerized by the countless wonders and endless landscapes now

available to my freshly opened eight-year-old eyes. Indeed, there was a brand-new bright and shiny world out there, just waiting for me to see, to experience, to explore.

However, in spite of my previous lack of visual perception, I honestly remember feeling no remorse at having learned that I had been "missing out" on so much for so long. Because, while the other kids with 20/20 vision were seeing the blackboard, television screen, and far-off scenery with perfect clarity, I was busy beholding other things. In essence, an entirely different universe ...

For early on, long before getting glasses, there had begun within me a deep fascination with the natural world, the dance of colors, the constant interplay between darkness and shadow and light. Being severely myopic, or nearsighted, I was unable to focus clearly on anything farther than six inches away. Therefore, all the forms and shapes and lines beyond that distance tended to mix together, blend, and join each other in one big blurry collection of colorations and glowing lights. Instead of many different things, subjects, and distances, all became just one thing, one subject, one distance. One—and only one—huge enormous resplendent cosmos surrounding me, enveloping me, immersing me. It was like being in the center of a colossal montage, or collage, or pointillist painting, only all hazy like a foggy morning, or seeing underwater, or peering through a stained-glass window. The visible stuff would intersperse with the invisible in my child's eye and become just "one stuff," not many different parts or pieces or puzzles. To me, everything was indistinct, thus connected.

Indeed, my first memory from earliest childhood is of me lying in a cradle in the bedroom by myself. I clearly remember gazing around the room at all of the blurry walls and windows and pictures, and then gradually everything would begin to melt together into a beautiful oneness. I would find myself looking *through* the visible world, and into what I believed to be the "real" realm, the one *behind* the walls.

Even now, forty-four years after receiving my first pair of eyeglasses, I sometimes like to remove them, for no apparent reason, and go back in time to the days of my youth. I enjoy seeing everything all nice and fuzzy once again. The way it used to be.

This daily experiment is roughly equivalent to the difference between surveying scenery through a clear picture window and then seeing the exact same scenario blurred by a heavy rainfall filming over the glass as it flows down the pane like luminescent wet paint lending a pleasing, glowing, neon quality to life that is just not there when I put the spectacles back on.

Yes, there is a genuine "cheap thrill," even ecstasy, even occasional enlightenment involved in the voluntary blurring of reality that inevitably occurs whenever I return in my mind's eye to the time and place where I first witnessed the world.

Childhood.

For back then there was a clarity and purity to life, in spite of the cloudiness caused by my "imperfect" eyes. A way of perceiving, of observing, of absorbing the primal essence of the universe unadulterated or altered or perverted by possessing "perfect eyesight." A certain type of vision that is only, wonderfully *only* available by using the two eyes that I was born with and will take with me into the grave. Just as they are.

When contact lenses first became popular in the 1970s, I never seriously considered getting them because the idea of installing foreign objects inside of my eyelids was anathema to me. Nowadays, of course, there are various forms of eye surgery that will "fix" most vision problems, including nearsightedness. However, I hesitate to have that operation because, again, I don't relish the thought of allowing outside influences—such as, say, laser beams—inside of my eyeballs. Besides, I have excellent sight right now. With, or without glasses …

Incredibly enough, there is a unique sort of insight that is acquired through having poor vision. A visual learning, or vivid imagination, or instinctual understanding of not only what is "there," but also what is "not there." A mental image, as well as optical. A seeing, a sensing, a savoring of lights and colors and auras as immaculate as the moment human eyes were created. A conception far beyond the merely material. Because, you must see, there are more planes of existence than only this single one.

Many more.

All life is illusion.
—Buddhist belief

Most, but not all, of the ideas, notions, and convictions that we believe in have arrived via the body's five main senses. In essence, we trust what we see, feel, smell, taste, and hear. And yet there are "other" things we place our confidence in, things which come to us in some fashion other than physically. The entities that have somehow evolved within the heart and soul rather than on the corporeal level, and therefore have no proven, solid, tangible, substantial evidence of their actual existence. Still we believe in them.

Perhaps there is a vision, or inspiration, or divine revelation that eventually comes to us somewhere along the dusty trail when we suddenly realize that there is more, oh so much more to this life than "meets the eye." A blurred vision, yes, but one which is even more ravishing than the "real world."

> *All this becomes a painting.*
> —Su T'ung-po

Recently I've been wondering if having weak eyesight is not really a handicap, minor curse, or even small disadvantage after all, but rather a blessing, of sorts, in disguise. Because without 20 over 200 vision, I would never be able to see the lovely scenery that I witness each and every time I take off my glasses, or go swimming, or wake up from a good dream. And yet am still in it.

Simply put, I have the best of both worlds now. Spectacles, or not. Focus, or blur. Reality, or so-called unreality. Either way, both of them have their place.

In my beautiful universe.

Road to Nowhere

Most roads go somewhere. That is, almost all byways and highways in this world were built with a definite destination in mind. The men who constructed them were charged with laying down a drivable route from point A to point B in as short a distance as possible. Whether an avenue connecting two streets in town, a gravel lane joining two growing villages out in the country, a steep four-wheel-drive trail zigzagging to a long-closed silver mine, or a freeway spanning the continent, practically every thoroughfare ever created had a specific goal or obvious intention, or at the very least, someplace to go.

But not all of them did.

For there are passageways that lead nowhere in particular, in fact, no place at all. They seem to just appear from out of the void, and then slowly but surely vanish back into it. They exit the main drag at some nondescript point and then begin to gradually fade into the dust, the sagebrush, the shadowy forest, the shimmering horizon. Having no rationale for existence, these spectral boulevards of the timeless zone are usually avoided by normal people who have a destination they wish to reach as soon as possible. Folks in a hurry, that is, the vast majority of Americans, typically stick to the paved roads, the state highways, the four-lane interstates in between cities.

However, not everybody loves speed, logic, efficiency, and straight stripes of asphalt conducting vehicles across the country like seventy-mile-an-hour conveyor belts. And so, for the rest of us, thankfully, there are back roads. This is the story of one of them.

In far southwestern Colorado, out beyond the ski resorts and golf courses, trophy homes and traffic jams, there is a dirt road that is listed as "C. R. 136" on the LaPlata County map. It leaves the main road just below Wildcat Pass and meanders toward the south and west for who knows how many miles. Most locals call it the "old road," or "south road," or "Long Hollow Road," or "the back way to New Mexico." One old-timer told me it was originally an Indian trade route between the mountain tribes of the north and the desert peoples of the south, that later outlaws used it to escape Colorado justice and head for the hinterlands, and furthermore that he and his buddies, fresh home from the war, had considered it their own personal racetrack when they first acquired cars back in the forties.

Now, while 136 road is a good place to drive fast—fairly smooth with few washboards or sharp turns—it is even more delightful to do it nice and slow. Low gear at ten mph is about right. Any faster and you will scare the wildlife, scatter the gravel, and raise a dust cloud visible for miles around. Any faster, and you might miss the reason why you came here.

When I first discovered this way I had no idea where it went, and still do not. One day while driving home from Durango, my trusty old pickup truck took a left turn at the right corner and just kept on going. Like a cantankerous yet wise mule, "Red" would often wander off in some mysterious direction like he knew where he was bound, so I would let loose of the reins just to find out where in tarnation we'd wind up.

On this particular occasion, our brand-new yet ages-old road soon crossed a dry arroyo and headed up the hillside to a wooded mesa. After only a mile or so I began to realize that this was no ordinary byway. Indeed, several hours later, back at my humble trailer in the boondocks, I knew that I had stumbled upon something special. Because, you see, a path that seemingly goes nowhere, yet always takes you home, is more precious and priceless than any parkway or turnpike on earth. And is certainly more pleasant …

Driving NE to SW down lonesome 136 there is very little traffic to encounter. Mostly ornery old ranchers, half-crazy oilfield workers, and odd couples in dusty black Cadillacs cruising the back way to Farmington after spending the day in Durango. Over the years, I stopped and talked with a number of those folks out there in the outlands, and never did meet a normal one (which is how I prefer it).

The terrain itself varies from sandstone hills to piñon/juniper woods to crusty terra cotta fields patiently awaiting the next rainshower. The 136 road basically follows the top of a ridge in between Long Hollow Creek and Iron Springs Gulch as it rambles and rolls toward the sunset in the southwest but never seems to quite get there. While gliding along on this magic carpet ride made of stone and bone and rubber, be sure and take time to enjoy the scenery. Watch the movement of trees in the forest. Revel in the open areas where there are 360-degree panoramas of heaven and earth in the form of mountains and mesas and canyons, electric turquoise skies and brilliant white clouds and charcoal-colored storm systems growing by the minute and highlighted by lightning. See the old barns and corrals and remnants of fences. Dig the abandoned homesteads, the automobile graveyards, the garbage dumps slowly returning to soil. Observe the ravens, jackrabbits, and circling buzzards. Drive at roughly the pace of a gently loping coyote. Roll down the windows and listen to the soothing sound of four tires on gravel and hardpacked dirt.

Notice there are no mile markers or warning signs out here, no speed limits or stoplights, no restrictions or restraints. Normal roads have plenty of those things. The one you are on has none.

Indeed, over time you come to realize that the best way to travel "the old road" is to do so freely, fearlessly, aimlessly, because no matter where you go on this trail is perfectly all right. Explore every side road that you can, and there are many, which head off in every possible direction like the branches of a cottonwood tree, but always end at the same spot. In fact, over the course of countless trips I would invariably get wherever I was going, no matter which path I took, but was not quite sure just how that happened.

Now, I have never followed this enigmatic avenue all the way to the end of the line. If there is such a thing. One rumor speculates that it joins the LaPlata Highway a couple miles north of the New Mexico border. Another source claims that it continues across the river and eventually leads to a fantastic complex of Anasazi cliff dwellings on the reservation which has never been open to non-Indians. Yet another legend states that this particular passageway has no terminus, no final destination, but rather goes on and on forever like the spinning of this planet, like the dreams of the Ancient Ones, like an eternal longing for the home that we might never reach. I don't know.

What I do know is that whenever I have no set route or time frame or journey's end in mind, the back road will always take me there. Because the essence of getting home is the actual odyssey itself, not the eventual arrival. And the way that you move is more important than how fast you are moving. And the finest road of them all is the one which goes absolutely nowhere, yet takes you right where you need to be.

Walking Backward

Horses are pretty smart animals, but they don't know everything. For instance, they do not realize we human beings possess the unique ability to walk backward. That is, until we show them.

One time while out for a stroll, I passed a field where six horses were grazing contentedly in the new spring grass and early morning sunshine. They had seen me come by before and normally paid me no mind.

However, on this particular day something was "different." On a whim, just for the heck of it, I decided to walk backward. Then, just as I turned around and continued strolling, now in reverse, the horses suddenly stopped grazing and stared at me. Six huge heads lifted as one, their large brown eyes watching me with obvious curiosity, as if I were performing some feat previously thought to be impossible. For here was a mere human, walking *backward*, by himself, in broad daylight, for no apparent reason. And furthermore, he seemed to be enjoying it!

No other species on earth can walk backward as well as Homo sapiens. While some animals can be trained to do so, such as dogs and donkeys and circus elephants, most are simply not built for reverse propulsion. But we are, and it makes me wonder how come.

There is a reason "why" for almost everything, and thus there must be one for why we men and women and even small children are blessed with this extraordinary knack for walking backward. Maybe even a number of reasons.

Let's start with the health benefits. When you are walking backward, you are providing a perfect counter-stretch for your entire body. For you are now using the opposite muscle groups as when you are walking "normally," thereby giving your forward muscles (and tendons, ligaments, joints, etc.) a pleasant break. This is especially useful, even blissful, during a long hike or cross-continent journey, but can be readily employed and easily enjoyed at almost any time and place, even during the shortest of rambles. Just find a level, straight, unobstructed pathway. Then turn around and proceed, now in reverse.

As you walk backward, allow your body to find the right pace, rhythm, and movement of body parts. Swing your arms. Swivel your hips. Roll your feet. "Heel-toe" walking becomes "toe-heel," which somehow tends to balance and realign the skeletal structure. Move easily, fluidly, delightfully. After a while, when you get the hang of moving backward on your own two legs, you begin to "look forward" to doing it. Why? Because it feels good.

But there are other, further, unexpected advantages to this odd but acceptable, simple yet simply outrageous activity. For when you walk backward, you are not walking blindly. You do not "see less," as it might "seem." In fact, you actually see more.

Allow me to attempt to explain. When you are walking backward, you are witnessing the world in reverse. Indeed, in the exact opposite of the way that you usually perceive it, which somehow reveals more to the naked eye than normal walking does. Let us compare the two.

As you walk forward, you are moving into the smaller picture that is ahead of you, while leaving the larger picture behind. Everything in your sight is, in essence, coming at you, which limits your capacity to see the whole canvas.

On the contrary, when you walk backward, you are constantly entering *into* the larger picture, the one right behind you, while everything is now coming into view, even as it is slowly moving *away* from you, instead of coming *at* you. Your range of vision gradually increases, the scenery literally enlarges before your very eyes, and your horizons expand with each and every new step that you take.

And receive.

For walking backward is not regressing into blackness. Rather, it is going forward into the darkness that is now becoming light. It is reversing the treadmill that then becomes a magic carpet ride. It is moving onward into the heavenly place that you have already been to. The paradise you will eventually return to.

If you wish.

Your goal is your starting place.
—Diamond Sutra

Society seems enamored with Progress. Always moving ahead, farther, faster, bigger, better. More, more, more! Change for the sake of change. Progress in the name of Progress.

I am not buying it.

For oftentimes it is wiser to slow things down, or stop them altogether, perhaps even reverse course. To return to a simpler, purer manner of living. To do things the old-fashioned way, just for the heck of it. In other words, because it is fun. Real fun, not the "virtual" kind. Enjoyment for the sake of enjoyment. Enlightenment for free, if you see.

So the next time you go for a saunter in the country, a hike along the beach, a trek across Nepal, try something different. Do the unusual. Blow some freaking minds. Human, equine, maybe even your own.

Walk backward. Slowly. Gracefully. Ecstatically. Indeed, stroll backward into Heaven. For Heaven is here on earth. Right here and right now.

Behind you.

The Movement of Trees in the Forest

Once you learn to see the space between the moving leaves of a
tree, an entire new world begins opening up.
—Dolores LaChapelle

Most Americans now spend practically their entire existence within
the confines of crowded cities and sprawling suburbs. Consequently,
we tend to live in boxes. Square boxes, rectangular boxes, boxes
with four corners, boxes with far more than four corners. We sleep
in boxes, ride in boxes, work in boxes, do our shopping at big box
stores, and come home at night to our own personal private boxes.
Apparently we are partial to the general design and dimensions of a
box, that is, four walls, a ceiling, and a floor, because we are almost
constantly surrounded by them. Kind of like coffins for the living.

It wasn't always this way. For, you see, the vast majority of
our ancestors knew nothing of boxes. They were utterly ignorant of
the ninety-degree corner, the perfectly straight line, the concept of
foursquare as opposed to round, the division between human nature
and nature, the desire to reside inside, and all the other inventions of
civilization and the recent industrial age. They lived outside, played
outside, worked outside, hunted outside, cooked their meals outside,
made love outside, even gave birth outside. When night fell or bad
weather came, they retreated to their caves, alcoves, pithouses, earth
lodges, igloos, tipis, and yurts, that is, circular rooms adopted or
constructed to keep the rain and snow and wind away.

But mainly they preferred "the great outdoors," long before
there was such a phrase in our language. They lived in the hills,
the mountains, the valleys, the meadows, the primeval forest, the
blessed sanctuary of Mother Nature rather than a two-bedroom
condominium surrounded by other two-bedroom condominiums.
To them, being cooped up all day in a square box with no access to
earth and heaven would have been akin to being caged and separated

from their family. Because at our deepest, grandest, most essential core, we human beings are more like wild animals than programmed automatons, more like wolves than genetically modified sheep, more like eagles than pet parakeets.

Somewhere along the evolutionary path we strayed from one lifestyle to quite another. We developed a fondness for safe, logical, predictable things. Vertical walls, horizontal ceilings, bubble-flat floors, double-locked doors, and windows that will not open. Lines, borders, boundaries. We came to rely on luxuries. Electric lights, central heating, air conditioning, running water, microwave ovens, remote controls, inside outhouses. We decided we liked being boxed in better than being outside.

Indeed, an ever-expanding percentage of people expend almost all of their precious allotted time on this spectacular planet deep within the bowels of buildings. Offices, factories, apartment houses, department stores, shopping malls, restaurants, hospitals, hallways, restrooms, elevators, closets, jail cells. They are born in boxes, live in boxes, die in boxes, get buried in boxes, and rarely venture very far away from their supposed comfort and security. In fact, about the only contact most city dwellers have with nature is the dash in between the front door and the car door in the morning, occasional walk through the park, annual vacation to "the country," potted geranium on the windowsill, or wildlife program on television presented in "living color." Now contrast this current way of life with the way it used to be.

Imagine, if you will—remember if you can—the daily existence of a Pleistocene hunter, a Neanderthal cave person, even an early American pioneer. While he would go inside his log cabin, sod house, or hole in the rock wall for sleep or whenever necessary, by far the lion's share of his time was spent outside in the fresh air, the sunshine, the starlight, the moonglow, the morning mist, the afternoon warmth, the refreshing coolness of evening. He prowled through the jungle, the desert, the grassland, the wilderness, the wide-open spaces that spawned us with all of his physical senses fully alive and alert. He felt the ground with his bare feet, smelled the air with his every breath, tasted the plants with his tongue and teeth, listened closely to the surrounding symphony, and witnessed the workings of the cosmos on an intimate, thoroughly engrossed, everyday basis. He observed the movement of cycles, circles, seasons, planets, clouds, birds, insects, animals, migrations, water, wind, fire, birth, death, and continuous rebirth. For there is so very much to see, to perceive, to experience, to appreciate in this vast and wondrous world, especially if we are able to revert to our former nature and think "outside of the box."

For instance, notice the various motions of a tree. Something so seemingly stationary and firmly rooted in the ground yet possesses a surprising amount of mobility. Indeed, the ways in which a tree moves are numerous and diverse.

First of all, there is the gradual growth from tiny seed to emerging sprout to established sapling to full maturity and ultimate fruition, that is, the production of seeds. Then comes the inevitable decline, perhaps disease, and surely death, followed by decay, descent, decomposition, and the graceful slow-motion metamorphosis from solid wood into soft dirt, into fertile bedding material, into the ideal incubator for the next generation of trees.

In between seedling and soil an average tree undergoes a wide assortment of movements, activities, and occurrences. See it sway in the breeze, dance in the wind, and jitterbug during the tornado. Watch an evergreen droop in the rain shower, the heavy snowfall, the overnight ice storm. Then watch it fluff back up like a pillow when the sun comes out, its limbs stretching and rising like arms in praise of the life-giving sky. Observe the deciduous trees growing new buds every spring, which quickly develop into an elaborate green velvet robe covering the upper two-thirds of the plant. As summer turns into autumn and the chlorophyll seeps out of the leaves, notice the foliage slowly change from jade, olive, kelly, emerald, and aquamarine to orange, scarlet, burgundy, yellow, and brown. Watch how the motley colors fall to the ground and fade into shades of gray. See the dark and gloomy forest of December become a winter wonderland in a matter of minutes during a blizzard, then switch back to black by the very next sunny day.

Notice how things are added and subtracted from a tree over the span of its lengthy lifetime. The acquisition of moss and lichen, spiderwebs and larva cocoons, bird nests and beehives, squirrel homes and hummingbird beds, antler markings and bearclaw scratches, woodpecker holes and charcoal black crowns left from long-ago lightning strikes. The loss of needles, twigs, branches, and layers of bark. The dropping of apples, acorns, walnuts, coconuts, piñon nuts, pistachio nuts, pecans, pine cones, poplar pollen, black locust pods, purple mulberries, blue cedar berries, pink cherry blossoms, and snowy white cottonwood seeds sailing on the breeze like miniature parachutes carrying precious cargo.

Observe the manner in which an aspen grove emerges from the blackened soil after a wildfire like a lime-green phoenix, its root system snaking underground like invisible vines and popping out every ten feet or so. See how it slowly but steadily marches across the barren valley floor and up the hillside, transforming the landscape in a matter of mere decades.

Watch a large healthy tree during a powerful storm, the waving limbs, the fluttering leaves, the swaying fruit, the bouncing motions, the fluid choreography, the balance, the symmetry, the unconscious grace, the simple and ecstatic joy of the dance.

Now let us slow things down, and take a look at the movement of trees from yet another perspective. Let us go for a walk in the woods.

Picture yourself strolling through a virgin forest on a calm, sunny, perfect summer day. There are both coniferous and deciduous trees on all sides in various shapes and sizes. As you leisurely move among them, you become increasingly aware that they are also in motion. Nearby trees dissipate into the background while those that were far off a few minutes ago become near. Trees to the left and right move at a speed roughly correlating to their distance from you. The closest ones are fairly fast while the midrange ones are somewhat slower and the farthest ones appear to be barely budging. A Douglas fir within arm's reach passes quickly by, while a blue spruce one hundred yards away is only slightly in motion, and an eighty-foot-tall lodgepole pine on a distant hill seems as dead-still as a tombstone.

Notice how the juxtaposition of individual trees is constantly changing as you wander through the forest. A sugar maple that was just a small blur like a drop of paint on a canvas becomes a unique and fantastic creation the closer one approaches. Then as you pass, it gradually disappears into the ocean of sun-dappled foliage like an object in the rearview mirror of a speeding car. See how trees go behind one another and vanish for several seconds, as if purposely hiding from your sight, only to reappear like magic on the other side. Watch as certain specimens catch your eye and come into vivid focus, even as others blend into the scenery like the pieces of a quilt. Note the many different shades of green and brown as they all mix together into a mural, a montage, a masterpiece of green and brown.

See the branches, twigs, and leaves of each and every hemlock, hickory, and hackberry as they twirl around the trunk like a slowly spinning ballerina. See the smaller trees frolicking like children beneath the watchful gaze of the elders. Now see them all together like members of a happy, vigorous, harmonious tribe.

But don't just utilize your 20/20 vision during this enjoyable ramble through the woods. Let your other senses loose as well. Smell the invigorating fragrance of pine, faint odor of oak, and sheer perfume of juniper resin. Touch the smooth paper-like bark of a white birch with your fingertips, rub your palms over the hard scaly skin of a ponderosa, caress the rough and deeply furrowed epidermis of the mighty cottonwood. Do something wild, crazy, even outlandish. Allow yourself to actually, literally, physically "hug a tree." Go ahead, nobody's watching.

See how it feels.

Now open your ears, your other, older ears, and listen to the delightful sounds of the natural world, so very different from the hectic, desperate, blaring noises of the human realm you left behind when you entered the forest. Hear the robin sing, the raven caw, the rabbit running through the brush. Hear the squirrels chatter, the sparrows scatter, and the bumblebees buzzing by. Hear the buck snort, the owl screech, the breeze blowing through the hollow, the stream whispering in the shallows, the pair of bluejays gossiping in the sycamore tree.

Sense the presence of unseen creatures watching as you travel past their well-hidden abodes. Feel the ancient sensation of being sheltered, protected, indeed, *embraced* by the spirits who dwell here. Imagine the fairies that must exist in this shady, shadowy, mysterious world, the wood nymphs lurking behind each bush, the invisible angels who inhabit enchanted places such as this.

Enjoy your splendid journey back in time, into the not-so-distant past, into the very crucible that helped to forge and mold and shape the human race, human psyche, human history. For this bizarre, ever-busy, ever-maddening contemporary lifestyle that so many of us have adopted does not afford numerous opportunities to escape the hustle and bustle, the racket and clutter, the pains and problems of boxes, big cities, backed-up freeways, and too many people clustered too closely together like laboratory rats. But your local Garden of Eden does.

Therefore, the next time you get a chance, break the monotonous spell of modern society and go for a nice long walk in the woods. As you saunter through nature's lovely cathedral, take a good look around you. For the slow-motion movement of trees in the forest is truly a soothing sight for weary, sorely civilized, once-animal eyes.

A Day Without Wind

Anyone who likes wind has never experienced it.
—Dolores LaChapelle

Years ago, while passing through the seaport of Sitka in southeastern Alaska, I heard a local joke about the region's infamous, incessant, cloudy, rainy, miserable weather. A tourist sees a little boy fishing on the dock and asks him, "When is the last time you had a sunny day around here?" The kid looks up and replies, "Gee, I don't know. I'm only seven."

That's pretty much the way I feel about the weather in the western half of America. Only it is not constant rain, or snow, or even cloudy days that bedevil us around here. It is wind.

Good old wind.

Think about it. Everywhere we go "out here" in the west is windy. It is windy on the Great Plains, where I grew up. It is windy in the Rocky Mountains, where I have spent most of my life. It is windy all along the West Coast. It is windy up in Canada and down in Old Mexico.

Indeed, whenever anybody anywhere in the western half of North America gives me the old, "It sure is windy around here," I cannot help but respond by blurting out, "Oh, yeah? Well, name me one place where it is *not* windy. Come on. I dare you. Just one!"

Of course, they never can.

Because, you see, the whole entire "left side" of America is windy. And I don't mean just kind of breezy. No, I mean WINDY. Windy as hell. Windy as a career politician. Windy as a typhoon on the Indian Ocean. Windy as a windmill in a hurricane. Windy like a cheap kite in a wind tunnel.

It is windy from west Texas to eastern Washington, from North Dakota to Southern Cal, from New Mexico to old Montana, from Nebraska to Alaska, and from the lowlands of Arizona to the high country of Idaho. And just about every place in between. (Old joke: Why is western Colorado so windy? Because Utah sucks.)

Plus, on top of all the normal everyday winds that plague this part of the world, we also get tornadoes in Kansas, cyclones in South Dakota, whirlwinds in Wyoming, dust devils in Nevada, and gale-force tempests on the Oregon coast. Everywhere that I have ever been to, there is wind. Wind, wind, and more wind.

The original four-letter word.

Now, wind is the worst weather condition of them all, at least to folks who work and play outside on a regular basis. It is the one thing that will ruin your day for sure. Because you can adapt, and adjust, to just about anything that you encounter in the great outdoors except for wind. If it's cold, you dress warm. If it snows, you put on a parka and wear snow boots. If it rains, you put on a poncho and wear mud boots. If it's hot, you go half-naked, drink ice-cold beer, and stay in the shade. But with strong, persistent, maddening, drive-you-crazy wind, there is absolutely nothing you can do about it except get out of it. In other words, go inside.

Ahh, much better.

During my lifelong hate affair with high winds, I have been darn near blown off of haystacks, mountain ridges, railroad bridges, telephone poles, and the rooftop of a tall building while carrying a sheet of plywood. I have been sandblasted by the wind in the desert. I have been stalked by the wind in the forest. I have felt the full force of the unfeeling, unrelenting, unforgiving wind out on the prairie and out on the sea, high above timberline and down below in Death Valley. I have been frozen by the "Frost Giants" (north winds) in Alaska, hounded by the howling zephyrs of the Canyon Country, hammered by the Santa Anas in Los Angeles, and pushed offshore on my surfboard by a sudden, down-sloping east wind at Huntington Beach.

One time, while I was working on irrigation engines out in the panhandle of Oklahoma, a ferocious gust of wind lifted my brand-new ballcap right off my head and sent it sailing horizontally across a gray, dusty, barren field. It was hardly even touching ground as it headed southeast at a high rate of speed. Sprinting after it as fast as I could run, the runaway cap was still "gaining separation" and would have surely made it clean to Texas if not for the barbwire fenceline at the far end of the field. That's where I found my hat, no longer new, plastered to a fencepost like paint on a wall.

Even the cities out here are windy. Indeed, I am quite certain that Albuquerque, Reno, Fargo, El Paso, Pocatello, Grand Junction, and Cheyenne would all surely give Chicago a run for its money as America's "Windy City."

Not to mention Winnemucca.

Yes, this is godawful gusty country we got out here. As a matter of fact, anywhere west of the Missouri River is just plain and simple windy, or at least breezy, almost all of the time. And therefore, a day without any wind at all—imagine!—is a rare and precious godsend. As scarce as finding a needle in a haystack, or a diamond in a coalpile, or a spontaneous street party in downtown Provo.

Or a nice sunny day in Sitka, Alaska.

All of which are mighty few, and far between.

And so, the next time you walk out your front door, and are *not* greeted by a powerful blast of wild western wind right in the face, be sure and thank your lucky stars.

Because a day without wind "around here"—or anywhere—is heaven on earth.

Still Life with Cactus Flowers

After a mile or so it dawned on me that I was in the wrong canyon. The one I wanted was larger, deeper, and not so steep, thus more likely to support human life a thousand years ago. It was also a half mile further south, on the other side of a long, vertical, unclimbable sandstone wall. When my map-reading error became apparent, I considered backtracking to the bottom and going up the "right" route to the "right" place. But then my interest in the unknown and curiosity about blank spots on the map kicked into gear, and I decided to continue climbing up the canyon. For it was too late to turn back now.

This particular incident took place during one of my springtime visits to southeast Utah. Whether I was living in northern Utah or western Colorado, the desert always seemed the ideal spot to be come April and May, for it was such a sunny, warm, magical cure for the cold and snowy winter we had just endured in the mountains. These annual journeys to the canyonlands consisted of several days to several weeks of camping, hiking the spectacular backcountry, and searching for remnants of the Anasazi people who lived and worked and played here so many centuries ago.

Before vanishing forever.

Over the years I collected a number of maps covering a large portion of this strangely captivating land. Many of them were detailed topographical quadrangle maps printed by the United States Geological Survey in the 1950s and 1960s showing elevation contours, peaks, valleys, streams, jeep roads, etc. Some of the older ones even revealed where you could locate ancient Indian ruins (no longer the case with newer maps), and I quickly became fascinated with finding them, exploring them, and investigating the rise and fall of this enigmatic culture.

After thorough research, the experts believe that the first humans arrived in the Four Corners area around 8000 BC, agriculture about 1000 BC, and permanent surface structures (as opposed to simple pithouses) circa AD 800. The more elaborate buildings (castles, towers, cliff dwellings, etc.) were constructed during the Classic Pueblo Period of the twelfth and thirteenth centuries. This was a time of great material, social, and spiritual development for the people. Crops were abundant, game plentiful, building techniques evolving, and commerce with other tribes flourishing. Life was good. Then, around AD 1300, the entire area was abandoned.

Now, nobody knows for sure why "the Ancient Ones" left their villages behind, and the years and layers of dust and debris have covered things in such a way that modern archaeological methods will never expose. There are signs of overpopulation, civil unrest, warfare, pestilence, and exhaustion of natural resources (ring any bells?). But the main reason was most likely a severe and prolonged drought during the late 1200s which dried up the springs and sent the Anasazi migrating south to intermingle with the Hopi, Zuni, and Pueblo tribes of what is now Arizona and New Mexico.

However, one thing is absolutely certain. They did not leave southeast Utah and southwest Colorado for lack of scenic wonders.

And so, bright and early one sparkling spring morning, I headed up an east-facing canyon on the side of a massive sandstone ridge reaching high into the cerulean blue sky. I was hoping to find a group of cliff dwellings shown on my government map from 1962.

While the desert is oftentimes quite windy (especially during spring), it is just as often dead calm. Calm as the air in a vacant house, as the tea in a cup, as a valley on the moon. This was one of those days. Indeed, everything was so peaceful and surreal the landscape seemed to be in a state of suspended animation, as if I were strolling into a three-dimensional still life painting instead of a living, breathing, sentient world.

While hiking the lower draw I saw no recent sign of man, which struck me as rather odd, since most known Anasazi sites in this region were regularly visited by locals and tourists alike. However, instead of tire marks, boot prints, and beer cans, I observed only coyote tracks, squirrel scratches, and mouse trails in the sand.

I also noticed a variety of healthy wildflowers, including several yucca bushes that only blossom every seven years. But it wasn't until climbing a steep slickrock arroyo and arriving on the "second level" that I was treated to a sumptuous botanical feast for my sorely snow-blinded eyes. For here, there, and seemingly everywhere were hundreds of cactus plants in full, resplendent, mind-blowing bloom. Never before—and not since—had I been so blessed to witness such a splendid proliferation of desert flora in such bright, rich, brilliant hues. There were cactus flowers in shades of shiny canary and lustrous pink and vivid vermillion and violet red. Obviously I had hit the right spot at just the right time—in spite of being in the "wrong" canyon—and the arid badlands were magically transformed into what appeared to be a meticulously cultivated rose garden.

In the middle of the desert!

This stunning development soothed my earlier disappointment at learning of my route-finding mistake, and I found myself tickled to involuntary laughter with my decision to continue up the smaller, less promising canyon. Taking a break amid the unlikely color show, I temporarily forgot my quest for ancient ruins, and enjoyed my current once-in-a-lifetime bounty of visual delights. Little did I know at the time that I was about to stumble upon something even more astonishing. Even now, a decade later, my extraordinary discovery seems more like a dream than an actual memory, almost as if it did not really happen.

But it did.

After climbing to the top of the crest at five thousand feet, I ate lunch and reveled in the unrivaled scenery, the vertical rock, the views of distant mountain ranges named Blue, Henry, LaSal, LaPlata, and San Juan. Then I decided to risk taking a different route back down.

Traversing the airy ridgeline to the north, I eventually found another east-facing canyon that looked doable, so I dropped off the edge and began the descent. After a half mile or so, I saw a side canyon to the left that looked promising, if only because it was south-facing (the preferred location for cliff dwellings). Also, the bottom of the wash appeared to have had a spring-fed stream at one time, a prerequisite for living in this dry and thirsty land.

After bushwhacking through a tangle of brush at the lower end, I continued on, ascending in between sunshine and shadow and walls of sheer sandstone. Then, while rounding a corner that turned abruptly to the north, I saw it.

Holy shit.

For there, underneath a large pale overhang stained with watermarks, was a cluster of buildings tucked into a dark alcove like caulking stuffed into the crack of a log cabin wall. I froze in my tracks, as if suddenly trespassing, and instinctively listened for sounds. There were none.

Quietly approaching the ledges of slickrock, talus, and prickly pear cactus leading up to the yawning entrance of the cavern, I found myself wondering when the last living human being had visited this secret, isolated, well-hidden place. It was surely not lately, as my footprints in the sand were the only recent evidence of mankind.

Leaving the intense Utah sunlight and entering the cool, shady cave, I felt a sense of awe, an aura of enchantment, a sensation of pure bliss come over me like I always do whenever finding a waterfall, gold mine, or ghost town not shown on the map or listed in the guidebook. I moved slowly, silently, respectfully, so as to honor the peace and beauty and sacredness of this solitary site.

There were several dozen rooms, now roofless, dilapidated, and connected by crumbling walls composed of rock, mortar, and smooth half-petrified wooden beams. There was a caved-in kiva (circular underground chamber used for religious ceremonies), a round three-story tower, and an upper building on a side cliff that seemed inaccessible without a tall ladder (possibly their "safehouse" in case of attack). There were a number of astounding petroglyphs carved into the rock walls, including an elaborate swirling spiral that ended in a series of mountain peaks. There were pictographs of bighorn sheep, deer with large antlers, and owls with enormous eyes, plus red and white handprints painted high on the stone face above the cliff dwelling (again, only reachable by wooden ladder or perhaps rope). There were bizarre images of broad-shouldered horned "gods" hovering in space as if guarding this mysterious place from whomever might disturb it.

I found various pieces of pottery (some ornately decorated in geometric designs), several metates (grinding bowls used for making flour, cornmeal, etc.), and numerous primitive tools, sharp stones, pointed bones, and animal teeth. I discovered tiny corncobs, long dekerneled by rodents, stashed into cracks at the rear of the cave and partially sealed off by form-fitting pieces of beveled sandstone. In one rectangular room there were flakes of flint, agate, quartzite, obsidian, even seashells.

A thousand miles from the ocean.

For you see, these prehistoric "Indians" (or Native Americans, or Anasazi, or Ancient Ones, or Ancestral Puebloans, or whatever term is currently politically correct) were a sociable and industrious lot, and maintained trade lines stretching all the way from west Texas to the West Coast, and from northern Utah to northern Mexico. They were excellent craftsmen and imaginative artists, bartering their goods (pottery, pelts, beads, etc.) with far-off tribes for items such as cotton, copper, turquoise, abalone shells, and parrot feathers that were not available in southeastern Utah.

While gently exploring what had once been home, sweet home to a small tribe some eight hundred years ago, I got the distinct impression that these people were happy, healthy, creative souls in perfect tune with their environment. Although existing in a sparse and unforgiving landscape, they had nonetheless managed to forge a beautiful lifestyle perhaps best epitomized by how well their architecture blended in with the surrounding scenery. Indeed, unlike modern man, their homes, workplaces, and gardens were hardly discernible from what nature had placed there before they arrived from the north, so many moons ago.

After a while, I stopped climbing around and peering into places where I perhaps did not belong. I sat down cross-legged in the center of the ruins and listened to the silence, and then to the music.

In between the songs of the canyon wrens, the caws of the ravens, the cries of the soaring hawks, and the sudden rush of a dive-bombing cliff swallow, I pretended to hear voices, laughter, babies, dishes in the kitchen, dogs barking, turkeys gobbling, flutes playing, and spring water dripping down from above into a stone cistern. I imagined hearing the divine melody at its most sublime, which is the sound of human beings communing with Mother Nature. I pictured a place of stark beauty and simple charm, stillness and tranquility, grace and perfection. I envisioned a desert Shangri-la, far, far from the maddening crowd, that the very gods themselves had made "just so." I visualized a way of life where there was no distinction made between human nature and wild nature.

Because there was none.

After allowing my mind to wander for a pleasant long while, I came back to the present, and yet felt as if still in a daydream of the distant past. For floating in the air all around me now were countless dust motes stirred up by a passing breeze, which somehow seemed to be the spirits of the people and creatures and kachinas that inhabited this earthly yet heavenly realm so very long ago.

The time spent at the abandoned village in the middle of nowhere passed by in a mystical trance until I noticed that it was late afternoon and time to go. I returned the miniature corncobs to the crack and placed the rocks back where they were. I left everything as it was, as it should be, as it hopefully remains: lost, timeless, eternal.

Just before leaving, I said my traditional farewell blessing out loud, the first words spoken all day. The sound of my voice occupied the alcove, but only slightly, only momentarily, and then was gone. All was silent once again.

I hoisted my pack onto my shoulders, closed the door behind me, and headed down the canyon that was now filling with shadows.

Patient as a Predator

One day during late December I parked my pickup truck on the west end of the dam at Vallecito Lake in southwestern Colorado. Just before heading out for an afternoon hike along the sunny east shore, I was getting my pack ready when I noticed something out of the corner of my eye. For there was a conspicuous black-and-white object on the mostly frozen lake, right where the growing ice sheet of winter met the still open water of autumn.

At first I thought it was just a dark tree stump or something with a clump of fresh white snow on top. But then, after a couple more glances, it started looking like a bald eagle, sitting perfectly still on the edge of the ice, waiting for a fish to come by. Not having my binoculars with me, I could not tell for sure which one it was. Eagle or stump. Stump or eagle. And so, while walking east across the dam in the sparkling new snow, and then north up the shoreline through the woods, I kept one eye on the figure out on the lake. From some spots overlooking the area, it appeared to be just an old tree stump. And yet, from other vantage points, I could have sworn that it was a real, live bald eagle, sitting there, "fishing."

Oh, so patiently.

Now I have always been amazed at how absolutely stock-still wild animals can be, for tremendously long periods of time, when they are hunting, or when they are being hunted. Indeed, it often comes down to a waiting game to see which one, predator or prey, gives away its position first. I once observed a golden tomcat in my garden, hidden among the flowers, who spent a good solid hour watching the flocks of sparrows as they would come and go through the rows of tomatoes and peppers and corn. He did not move, one bit, the whole entire time. In fact, the only motion that I noticed at all was in his eyes as he ever so patiently spied on the yummy morsels of food flying by just a few short feet away. Then, finally, one poor little bird swooped down a tad too low, and the hungry cat finished him off with one lightning-swift leaping claw.

94

One other time, I was walking through the aspen forest on the northwest shore of Electra Lake. It was raining softly, and all was stone quiet except for the soothing sounds of water dripping from wet branches. All of a sudden, I came upon a deer, a nice healthy doe, standing on the far side of a small clearing. I instinctively froze on sight, and so did she.

The game was on.

Now, I was not hunting, and carried no weapon, and therefore she had no reason to fear me. However, I decided to conduct a little experiment. I wanted to see which one of us, man or deer, human or animal, civilized being or wild critter, could outlast the other in this contest of who moves first. So for the longest time (thirty minutes?) I did not move a muscle. And neither did she. Roughly fifty feet apart, the two of us just stood there in the morning rain, staring at each other. Neither one of us moving, or flinching, or even breathing very hard. I even tried as best as I could to keep from blinking my eyes (not easy to do—try it some time).

After a while, the completely motionless deer began to look more and more like a photograph or painting than an actual living being, and I started to wonder if I had somehow entered a time warp wherein everything was frozen solid. Finally, after what seemed like an eternity, as my normally mobile body felt like it was about to lock up, and my legs began to ache from the inactivity, I felt a cough coming on. I tried swallowing several times, but it was no help.

Then, just as the soft little cough escaped from my throat, the doe suddenly leapt into action and disappeared into the woods in a matter of mere seconds.

As if she had never existed.

On yet another occasion I was climbing in the Wasatch Range of northern Utah when I came up on a mountain goat. Normally it is quite rare to see one of these shy and elusive creatures, much less get close to one, but luck was with me that morning. For as I traversed the rocky ridge headed west for the lofty summit of Mount Superior, not only was the blinding sun rising behind me, but the wind was directly in my face. Therefore, the goat could not see me or smell me until I was very near. Hiding behind a big boulder, I peered around the corner carefully. Sure enough, he had heard me, or perhaps just sensed me, and was staring straight at me, his eyes and face intensely focused on mine. I froze like a February icicle.

Realizing that I might never get another close-up view like this one ever again, I took my time admiring the noble, awesome, legendary animal standing right there in front of my eyes. Likewise, the goat watched me intently and did not move either. After a while his grayish white fur began to blend into the grayish white color of the granite wall behind him. Then, as time stood still, and yet continued on unabated, his body began to "disappear," like a mandala when you stare at it long enough, and soon all I could see were his two black horns, two black eyes, and four black hooves.

All the while his gaze remained glued to mine, and I somehow got the feeling that we were now engaged in the ultimate staredown of all time, and furthermore that he was slowly winning, and even perhaps beginning to, well, hypnotize me.

And so, if only to break the spell, I decided to see if I could get even closer. Slowly ducking down behind the boulder, I crawled quietly along the ridgeline toward the beast. After only about fifteen seconds, I risked raising my head to see if he had moved yet. Yes, he had. Indeed, he was gone!

In fact, even though I could not distinguish any possible hiding places anywhere in sight, and had heard no hooves scampering across the solid stone, the magnificent mountain goat had completely vanished. As if into the thin air, as if he were a ghost who had left no evidence of his passing, as if he were just a figment of my imagination.

In any case, by the time I returned from my delightful hike in the newly fallen snow, I was convinced that there was no bald eagle on the ice after all. Surely no live bird could just sit there, immobile, for several hours on a cold winter day like that. And so, as I came back to my old pickup truck waiting for me on the dam, I tossed my pack into the cab and then remembered that I needed to check the oil. After doing so, I slammed the heavy metal hood with a loud bang. Just then, out of the corner of my eye, I saw something move…

And there, crossing the lake toward the far shore, flew a large, healthy, black-and-white bald eagle!

Yes, the "stump" was not a stump after all. That hungry bird of prey had spent three solid hours watching the surface of the dwindling open water, hoping to catch a nice big trout for supper before the lake froze up completely for the winter. And then I had come along, and thoughtlessly interfered with his hunt, and scared him away from his potential meal by making a loud noise in the utter stillness of the silent mountains.

Either that or he was just taking a nap and I woke him up.

The Doing of Dishes

Show me something that isn't magic. For it often occurs to me that we are literally surrounded by the sublime, the extraordinary, the ridiculously perfect. Every day, every hour, every moment. If only we take the time to notice.

Unfortunately, most Americans are in such a hurry that we tend to overlook the numerous chances to access the divine which are presented to us on a regular basis. Indeed, there are many seemingly mundane tasks in this fast-paced modern society which we relegate to machines that could easily become a daily blessing, a soothing meditation, an excellent opportunity to touch the heavenly if only we would do them ourselves, by hand, by simple human effort. For there is an ancient insight into the delicate workings of the universe to be gained by consciously relishing the earthy yet ethereal facets of work, of physical movement, of getting our hands dirty, of good old-fashioned manual labor.

For instance, people who rely on automatic dishwashers to clean their cooking and eating utensils are missing out on one of the most delightful activities on this ever-amazing planet: washing dishes. I kid you not. Because there is more, oh so much more to "doing the dishes" than meets the mortal eye. Therefore, to further understand this phenomenon, let us examine this supposedly boring job from beginning to end.

First comes the gathering of dishes and filling of the sink. Plug the drain and arrange the platters, plates, and silverware on the bottom. Now open the faucet and let the precious hot water pour out like an instant waterfall and mix with the soap to create a thousand white bubbles foaming like sea surf as steam rises to form a veil of almost-invisible silver molecules floating in the air in front of your face. Add bowls and glasses while immersing hands and wrists into warm liquid ecstasy as if you were stepping into a hot springs pool after a cold winter's day. Set pots and pans soaking on the side to do at the very last. Leave it all to simmer for a few minutes.

There.

Now reach for the sponge and begin. Consider the careful rubbing, the gentle wiping, the firm scraping necessary to get everything nice and clean. Notice the wonderful similarities between washing dishes and washing your hands, or bathing a baby, or massaging your lover's back. Observe the fluid grace involved, the velvet harmony inherent, the circular motions, the swirling waves, the miniature ocean now glowing in the golden morning light of your kitchen window. Watch as cups, lids, and ladles leave the soapy water dripping and move to the other half of the basin almost as if you were witnessing the blessed process rather than actively participating in it.

Listen to the musical noises the cheerful voices of the various utensils composed of porcelain and plastic and steel make as they fill the vacant side of the sink. Feel the comforting heat of the water as it ascends through your arms and disperses throughout your body. Allow the washing of dishes to cleanse your inner being simultaneously. For you are now permitted to approach the very source of all inspiration as you perform this humblest of chores.

When the wash side is empty except for dirty water, there comes the unplugging of the outlet hole and immediate commencement of the pool draining as it twirls merrily down, down the pipe and into a subterranean cavern. Then the faucet handle is turned on once again, just enough to enable a lukewarm trickle to flow like liquid diamonds across the shiny surface of the dishes as they are tenderly rinsed and placed one by one, just so, into the waiting drainer. Plates in back, cups and bowls up front, forks and spoons and spatulas in special holders, pots and pans on top.

Then you sponge down the counter, wipe wet hands with a towel, and witness the dishes drip drying due to gravity, air drying due to evaporation, and glistening like seashells on the beach after a storm.

Now allow the satisfaction of a job well done to sink in like the serenity of a sunny autumn afternoon in the Rocky Mountains. For when this daily duty, this enjoyable work, this childlike play is completed, you have done more than mere dishes. You have taken part in a ritual, a mysterious relationship between the menial and the divine, a sensuous form of enlightenment only available to those who get their hands dirty, or in this case, clean. Because, you see, the simple act of washing dishes, viewed properly, is nothing short of sheer magic.

Show me something that is not.

The Hands of God

So happy to be born
The baby opens
And closes his hands.
—Santōka Taneda

Shortly after we human beings learned how to walk on our two hind legs, everything changed. For it was then that the human hand began to form, develop, and metamorphose from a means of propulsion into the miraculous entity we possess today. For the uses, abilities, and ultimate possibilities of our hands are almost limitless now, and nowhere else in the known universe does there exist such a skillful, proficient, and blessed tool as the humble human hand.

As our front paw evolved into four distinct fingers and one opposable thumb, we were able to do all kinds of new stuff. Because, you see, the gift, the propensity, the capability to open and close our claws, to hold, to carry, to construct, to create things with our own two hands was essential in our evolution from animal kind to mankind. Indeed, the human hand literally shaped the human race. Its extraordinary dexterity gave birth to craft, culture, agriculture, a multitude of inventions, and even art, which is the appearance of beauty in forms that only Homo sapiens can produce, or what Willa Cather called "that irregular and intimate quality of things made entirely by the human hand."

Over the span of a few hundred thousand years, we learned how to use these unique implements of ours in a million different ways, and thereby came to manufacture all that we see before us today. The hand forever shifted our lives from mundane to magical and became not only helpful but indispensable. Therefore, let us explore this one-of-a-kind appendage, this incomparable marvel, this remarkable mystery of the cosmos that most of us take for granted, hardly notice, and rarely appreciate. Let's examine the "hand."

The word itself is a very old one and was used similarly by a number of ancient languages including Middle English, Anglo-Saxon, and Old German (pronounced "hant" in the latter). It is possibly descended from the Gothic term "hinthan," which means "to grasp." However, as we shall learn, the human hand can do more than merely grasp. For the list of things we can now accomplish with our bare hands is not only astonishing, but endless. Indeed, there is nothing else in the world that can achieve as much as our hands can.

Think about it. A human hand can paint a picture, sculpt a statue, and write a symphony down on paper. It can mold pottery from clay, shape a canoe from a tree trunk, and carve a pipe out of a deer antler. It can knead dough, sprinkle spices, and decorate a cake. It can give a baby a bath, comfort an injured child, and gently cleanse an infected wound. It can flip a coin, fly a kite, and build a castle out of sand. It can tie a bootlace, button a shirt, and unbutton a blouse. It can caress naked skin, stroke a thigh, and cause intense excitement.

With just the fingertips.

A human hand can throw a curveball, catch a fastball, bounce a basketball, spike a volleyball, and put English on a cue ball. It can toss a shotput, fling a discus, sling a Frisbee, and skip a flat stone a dozen times across a glassy pond. It can play bongo drums, strum a guitar, "tickle the ivories," and direct an entire orchestra. It can thread a needle, knit a wool sweater, and hand stitch a homemade quilt. It can sharpen a knife and swing an axe and roll a cigarette. It can milk a cow and clean a fish and fix a barbwire fence. It can strike a match and start a fire.

Then put it out.

The human hand can soothe a fevered brow, massage tired muscles, and warm a half-frozen hummingbird back to life. It can pet a dog, fondle a cat, and brush a horse's mane. It can free a butterfly caught in a spider's web. It can clear a garden, dig a hole, plant a seed, pick a tomato off the vine and bring it to your mouth. It can stir the stew, serve the food, scrape the plate, wash the dishes, and put them away. It can turn a key, open a door, and close a window. It can change a diaper, fluff a pillow, and give a guy a pat on the back. It can splash water, it can make a snowball, it can melt ice. And that's not all.

The human hand can talk.

That's right. It can say all sorts of things, from hello and welcome to goodbye and so long. It can tell everybody who is number one, and who is not—with just one finger. It can wave, beckon, salute, point, and signal. It provides a beautiful language for those unable to speak, and reading ability to the blind. It communicates through the written word via newspaper accounts that change your mind, books that transform your life, and poems that rip your heart out. It writes love letters in longhand that are saved in drawers, tenderly opened, and cherished forever.

Why, the list is unlimited. For the ever-ready, ever-useful, ever-amazing human hand can do whatever is necessary. It can become a cup to scoop water out of a stream to drink from when you're thirsty. It can wash your face, rub your belly, scratch your itch, and wipe your bottom clean. It can carry a handbag, hand out handbills, play handball, produce handicrafts, fold a handkerchief and place it in your pocket just so. It can push a handcart across the prairie, propel a handcar along the railroad tracks, and steer the handlebars of a bicycle. It can hold on to a handrail, handpick an orchard, hand off a football, and help the handicapped. It can shake another hand in greeting, set the hands on a clock, and measure the height of an animal by how many "hands" it is. It can perform unbelievable tricks of magic by sleight of hand, for truly "the hand is quicker than the eye." It can even catch a fly!

It can let him go.

You can lend a hand, give a hand, get a hand, or ask for one in marriage. You can become an old hand, and therefore have a hand in important decisions. You can hand in an assignment, hand over the goods, and spend money hand over fist. You can play a hand of cards wisely and win hands down, or lose the game beforehand by showing everybody your hand. You can be handy, and handle problems promptly, or let them get out of hand. You can throw up your hands and quit, or join hands with others and succeed. You can have the upper hand, even a heavy hand, or you can wash your hands of such behavior.

On the one hand, we can use our hands to promote peace, while on the other hand we can utilize them for violent purposes. For the hand of man is capable of so much good and yet so much evil. Ultimately, of course, it is we humans who decide which. But remember this: Hands were not intended to hurt, but rather to heal. They were not made to hit, but rather to hold. They were not meant to attack, but rather to protect. They were not designed to destroy, but instead to create.

This is never more evident than when an artist's paintbrush moves across the palette and then the canvas, when a potter's palms and fingers form a bowl at the spinning wheel, when two lovers are walking hand-in-hand, when a grandmother picks up a crying infant with just the right "touch."

The human touch.

For there is a special warmth, magnetism, electricity, primal energy, and innate holiness within human hands. Witness the way they instantaneously assimilate themselves to whatever surface they touch, so apparent when "one hand washes the other." For the hour is now at hand for us to fully realize how very gifted our hands are, and behave accordingly.

In ancient Tibet, when a person was on the verge of dying, family and friends would gather around, "lay hands" on the body, and pray the spirit into the next life during the last hour, last minute, last moment of existence. In this way, the living could touch the divine.

Through their hands.

Yes, the hand of Homo sapiens is quite the singular creation. So capable, so sensitive, so sentient, so alive, so aware, so responsive, so giving, so caring, so sharing, so compassionate, so instantly comforting, so distinctly and utterly *human*. Indeed, the human caress feels so soft and soothing and skin-tingling that it seems almost heavenly, and is perhaps tangible proof of God's presence right down here on earth.

In closing, we need to "hand it" to the hand, the good old human hand. For it can do so very much, including all of the wonderful things just mentioned, plus at least a million more. Why, it can even write—handwrite, of course—an essay about itself.

An Oasis in Space

Suppose this is the only one.

Imagine, for just a minute, that this planet called Earth is the only one in the whole entire solar system, whole entire Milky Way Galaxy, whole entire Universe where the miracle of life as we know it is found, or likely, or even possible. It's not difficult to do. Because, you see, life is pretty rare.

Think about it. After all of our space missions, and moon landings, and NASA experiments, and high-powered telescopes, and high-definition satellite images of other planets, and supersensitive sensors sent far out into the outer reaches of space, and the billions of dollars spent on exploring what's "up there," no one in the ultra-intelligent human race has ever found conclusive proof that any form of life exists anywhere else in the Universe. Or ever did. Or ever will.

Now most people, myself included, believe that there is other life out there, that the miracle of life is not limited to this single small world alone. But I do have a theory to propose:

This is the only one.

Planet Earth is the only planet like this. This is the only place in the whole pantheon of sky gods, in the complete smorgasbord of celestial objects, in the entire galaxy of galaxies where life like THIS exists. For this is a magical oasis, indeed *the* magical oasis of all, the only one, and there is none other like it anywhere, anywhere, anywhere. No. This one, my friends, is special.

For only here, right here, did Father Sky supply all of the one million and one necessary ingredients for Mother Earth to somehow evolve, flourish, and develop into what we see before us today, even while in the very midst of cold, dark, lifeless space. Only here did the Universe produce and provide us with rainclouds and waterfalls and hot springs and perfect double rainbows. Only here are there rainbow trout, and peacocks, and butterflies, and flying squirrels. Only here—only here!—are there tropical forests, and sandstone arches, and greenish-blue glaciers, and vegetable gardens, and muffins in the oven, and powder skiing, and children playing on playgrounds, and schools of dolphins swimming in the ocean, and bald eagles flying through the sky, and laundry drying on the line, and smoke rising from a campfire, and laughter leaping from a hundred throats all at once, and bacon and eggs for breakfast down at the diner on Saturday morning.

All while spinning and twirling and hurtling through the vast lostness of the endless cosmos at thousands of miles per hour!

No, I guarantee you. This is the only planet like this. This one is unique. This one is sacred. And the human race had better not destroy it. Because this world is quite possibly the one and only pearl, the singular diamond, the solitary oasis in space, the Garden of Eden of all the galaxies. Indeed, our own little paradise incarnate. Call it Heaven, if you will, if you want.

Some scientists, some space experts, some "astrobiologists" now believe that the long list of extraordinary conditions that exist here on Earth are almost impossible to replicate or repeat elsewhere in the Universe. First, you would need a planet of just the right mass, orbiting at just the right distance from just the right star, itself at just the right distance from the center of the galaxy. It would be essential to have the proper amounts of gases and solids, liquids and metals, volume and weight, crust and core. You would require optimal levels of temperature and humidity, oxygen and carbon dioxide, gravity and velocity, electricity and magnetism. You would want things like volcanoes and earthquakes and the occasional asteroid hitting home. You would hope for a perfectly protective atmosphere, and large, sheltering planets revolving nearby. You would find it necessary for a tremendous supply of microbial life forms, that is, consummately reproductive seeds and supremely adaptive organisms from somewhere that were somehow fated, or meant, or intended to land here, and sprout here, and grow here.

Only here.

And last, but certainly not least, you would have to have a moon, one single satellite, of "just the right" size, circling at "just the right" speed, and "just the right" distance from this absolute, perfect, rarest gemstone of all the jewels in the sky. For starters.

So you see, we humans, we intelligent beings, we highly evolved configurations of animation live in a pretty special place. A pretty specialized little corner of the cosmos, which perhaps, just perhaps, is the only spot anywhere where Life found a foothold, fertility, and fruitfulness. Where Life encountered an incubator, a warm cradle, a magical crucible, a marvelous canvas, and, ultimately, a place to play.

Maybe Earth is so rare, so distinctive, so exceptional, so blessed, indeed, so divine for a reason. And what is that reason? We do not know. But just suppose ...

Suppose that this is the only one.

Life at Three Miles an Hour

All the shining angels second and accompany the man
who goes afoot, while all the dark spirits
are ever looking out for a chance to ride.
—John Burroughs

I'm kind of different. Different, as in old-fashioned. For instance, I have never been attracted to video games, fascinated with the latest electronic gadgets, or captivated by computers that accomplish things a million times faster than the human brain can. For that is too fast.

Likewise, I am not likely to ride somewhere in a car when I can just as well walk there. For to ride is easy. Too easy. While to walk, ahh, to walk is divine …

Indeed, the simple act of walking—putting one foot in front of the other without falling down—is perhaps the most underrated activity in the entire world. For several reasons.

Think about it. We humans are the only creatures on earth who really, truly "walk." Other animals crawl and creep and run and leap and scamper and hop and gallop and trot and fly and swim. But Homo sapiens is the only one who normally walks, upright, one step at a time.

On his two hind legs.

Somewhere way back in time, human beings stood up. And stayed up. And learned how to use their front paws for more than just propulsion. Then they learned how to carry things, make things, and use things. In essence, the ability to walk freed us from merely moving around, and allowed us to create, to invent, to become. It gave us a much larger palette, and a much wider canvas to paint on.

Nowadays walking comes to us naturally. When we are young, very young, walking is the first thing we want to learn to do. Some primal instinct stirs within us, and without any provocation at all we yearn, we long, we strive to stand up on our hind legs, without any help, and take a step. A first step. And then another, and another, and so on, until we are actually, physically, gloriously WALKING.

For walking, good old walking, is essential to the human race. This fact is never more apparent than when we become sick, or injured, or grow old, and we are faced with the grim prospect of not being able to walk. Indeed, most folks never truly value this priceless ability they possess until it is no longer possible for them to perform.

Walking is not only our main method of locomotion, but also our finest form of exercise. "Stretching the legs" tones the entire body, circulates the blood, strengthens the heart, develops the lungs, massages the organs, aids in digestion, and helps us to sleep at night. However, this wonderful little activity is not only beneficial for our physical well-being, but goes far beyond that. Because, you see, walking is also therapeutic for our "other side."

I know of no bodily movement that so effectively clears the mind and soothes the soul as walking. For the simple yet powerful act of traveling on foot affects your perception of reality as surely as water affects a fish.

Indeed, the motion and repetition, unconscious balance and miraculous fluidity, momentum and flow of walking tends to cleanse our view of the cosmos, allows us to see beyond the minor problems of this temporary existence, and enables us to perceive the larger picture, the whole picture, the sum of all the parts, not just a few fleeting pieces of the puzzle.

Somehow, when we manually transport our bodies forward, one step at a time, the physical exercise and constantly changing scenery serves to stimulate some primeval healing salve that lies dormant within us until we awaken it with a good long walk. In other words, we move, and the universe moves with us. We swing our arms and swing our legs, we increase our breathing speed and raise our heart rate, the juices begin to flow, the eyes start to revolve, the mind accustoms itself with Mother Nature once more, and suddenly we feel in tune again, in time again, in rhythm again with what is. Really is.

Indeed, the grand scheme of life is at its most intimate and enjoyable when we get outside and walk, and is simply not available to those who ride in automobiles or stay inside and watch it on TV.

Furthermore, when you walk you are ultimately FREE (or should be). You can go anywhere you want. When you are a true walker, foot-loose and fancy-free, you are not restricted to highways and roads like vehicles, nor railroad tracks like trains, nor an assembly line like a piece of a machine. Because when you are "on foot," you see more, hear more, smell more, feel more, sense more. You are more in touch with everything, and therefore allowed insight into the workings of the world, the secrets of the cosmos, the pace of the universe, indeed, the speed of life. Which happens to be about three miles an hour.

Yes, we were meant to walk. And so we should. For the ability to walk, to walk well, is nothing short of magic. Holy people down through the ages have recommended the simple, humble, *human* act of walking as a way of achieving enlightenment, understanding, and even heaven right down here on earth. For untold centuries, sages and mystics, saints and prophets, healers and philosophers have suggested that a good long walk is akin to meditation in motion, a pilgrimage to the inner soul, even a moving prayer, if you will.

Likewise, creative people such as artists, statesmen, and writers have discovered that going out for a stroll will almost always improve their focus, brighten their mood, and fix their problems whenever they find themselves stumped. In fact, numerous paintings, powerful speeches, and important chapters of famous books have appeared as if out of thin air following a brisk thirty-minute walk.

So take a walk. And see what "happens." Move those hips, legs, ankles, feet, and toes. Swing your arms, open up your lungs, and enjoy the electric panorama that changes with each and every step. Allow your breathing to synchronize itself with your stride. Keep moving. Keep rolling. Keep flowing. Like water in a stream.

You can tell a lot about people by watching them walk. Because how you walk reveals a great deal about yourself. Your gait, your stride, your bounce, your spring in the step (or lack thereof). The way you hold your head and shoulders, how you time your hands with your feet, how you approach the world. In fact, your personality, health history, and general outlook on life is conspicuously exposed by the unique way that you walk. In essence, walking is body language at its most expressive. And so, if you desire to be well, you must learn how to walk well.

Like an animal …

Watch how a wild creature moves. So fluid, so graceful, so meaningful. In curves, arches, and circles. For they do not walk in straight lines and squares like civilized people and robots do. They move more like water, like a gentle breeze, like a snowflake falling from the sky.

So slow down, my friends. Unless there is urgency, or an emergency, there is no need to hurry. You do not have to go thirty miles per hour, or sixty, or ninety, to be content in this world. Indeed, living too fast is a direct deterrent to genuine happiness, for when you are moving too rapidly you are letting the very best things in life pass you by. Things like smelling roses, seeing rainbows, and watching sunsets. Things like pleasant sounds, pleasing textures, and soothing scenery. Things like a clear mind, a joyful heart, and a satisfied soul. Things like earthly delights, heavenly moments, and helpful angels. All of which avoid excessive speed as if it were a curse.

There is a reason we humans are able to walk upright, on our two hind legs, with such perfect balance, such exquisite coordination, such exhilarating grace, all at about three miles an hour. And what is that reason? So we can fully enjoy our short time on this lovely planet.

And not miss a blessed thing.

The Swallow People

One summer day while driving down a deserted back road in between Durango, Colorado, and the New Mexico border, I came upon a remarkable sight that caused me to pull over and park. I sat and watched in silent, open-mouthed amazement as a large swarm of swallows performed a pirouette above a pasture, several hundred of the tiny birds twirling together in apparent jubilation, in perfect synchronicity, in close proximity to each other yet never two of them colliding. It was a rousing, soul-stirring, stunningly beautiful display, like a living, spinning, delirious top, like a tornado of wings and feathers and excited chirping noises, like a seemingly impossible yet somehow choreographed dance. The avian hoedown went on and on, back and forth across the field, rising and falling like a single creature instead of many, until it gradually dispersed and the birds disappeared one by one into the neon turquoise sky.

No, I was not hallucinating on acid.

Actually, this incredible exhibit of swallows in mass celebration did not come as a complete surprise to me. For fifty years I have witnessed their aerial acrobatics and marveled at their swiftness, their agility, their ability to turn on a dime and give you change, their instant acceleration, their exquisite fluttering grace as they hover at the nest while feeding their babies mouth to mouth. For no man-made aircraft, no matter how sophisticated, will ever maneuver as well as a swallow, and perhaps only the hummingbird surpasses it among the bird family.

Swallows are born to move, designed for speed, and inspired by the God of Joy. They live their lives in a blaze of activity, in the brilliant sunlight between heaven and earth, in soaring flights of what appears to be sheer rapture, as if they were divine spirits sent to encourage us mortals to reach for the sky even though we cannot fly. I sometimes imagine that swallows emerge from the ether, visit this planet for a few short years, and then return to their source of origination when they die (influenced by the fact that I have never found a dead adult).

Growing up in eastern Nebraska, I often spent weekends and part of each summer on my grandparents' farm. While we boys were allowed to roam the property carrying BB guns, Grandpa gently warned us "Never shoot a Barn Swallow." You see, swallows not only benefit farmers by eating harmful insects, but are the most beloved bird in all of Europe. My grandfather's parents came to America from "the old country" (Switzerland) where folks still build their homes with special roof eaves intended to attract the feathered angels that have been considered a sign of good luck since ancient times. Indeed, the deliberate destruction of a swallow nest is believed to bring misfortune and even catastrophe upon the house and its inhabitants.

Here in the United States, there are six main species of swallows (Barn, Cliff, Tree, Bank, Rough-winged, and Violet-green), including several that are indistinguishable without binoculars. They have long pointed wings and usually a forked tail, with dark colors on the back and paler shades beneath.

Swallows spend most of their waking hours in the air, in the sky, in the skillful pursuit of flying insects. They normally nest in colonies varying in size from a pair of homes to several hundred. A sociable tribe, swallows often hunt and rest communally. If other birds approach their nest, they will aggressively defend it. More than once I have seen them noisily mob a hawk and chase it away, furiously pecking at its tail feathers like snapping scissors.

As for shelter, Barn Swallows choose elevated sites, especially man-made structures such as barns, bridges, and grain elevators to build their sturdy circular nests of mud and twigs. Bank Swallows favor excavating holes into riverbanks, gravel pits, highway cuts, seashores, and other steep embankments with soft earth. Cliff Swallows construct their gourd-shaped dwellings under the eave of a building or on the side of a rock face. Tree Swallows prefer a woodpecker hole or other cavity for their soft, feather-lined, cup-like nest.

Because they depend almost entirely on insects for food, when cold weather draws near and the bugs disappear, so do the swallows. They migrate south, sometimes in flocks of several thousand, and spend the winter in Central or South America. Come spring they return to their ancestral breeding grounds, often arriving on the same day each year, such as March 19 at the famous San Juan Capistrano Mission in California.

Moving to western Colorado shortly after high school, I found myself fascinated by the Violet-green Swallows that populate the canyons, cliffs, and lakeshores of the region during summer. These are the true daredevils of the animal world, dive-bombing at one hundred miles an hour inches from solid stone, sometimes so close to me I could feel the passing breeze on my skin. I would sit for hours upon a high point and enjoy the show as they raced through the heavens like arrows shot from compound bows. And no, they were not always feeding on bugs. Oftentimes it was quite obvious that they were just having fun, like Jonathan Livingston Seagull, only much faster.

Years later, I lived in an old shack overlooking Vallecito Lake and never tired of watching the superbly talented Tree Swallows as they frolicked in the sky. Indeed, on several occasions I observed a pair of the little rascals appearing to, well, fornicate in flight, their bodies literally trembling with ecstasy as they connected while airborne (which gives new meaning to the old airline slogan "Fly United").

At my current home east of Cortez, Colorado, I am blessed with a Barn Swallow nest underneath the uppermost roof of the house. The inconspicuous egg incubator, composed of dirt and sticks and saliva, is a marvel of engineering and defier of gravity as it sticks to the vertical surface as if the builders used glue instead of mere mud for mortar. Virtually impregnable to predators, it hangs fifteen feet above my front porch, thus allowing me to closely observe the comings and goings of the swallow people as they tend to their nest and raise their babies.

Although residing here less than two years, I have noticed certain patterns developing in the life cycles of these mysterious birds. Returning from their winter vacation in early April, the swallow couple starts fixing the nest and getting it ready for the fragile eggs by lining the pouch with downy feathers, golden straw, and strips of colorful plastic.

By late May, the chicks have hatched (usually four), and I find pieces of eggshell (white with black speckles) lying on the front stairs. Soon there are small black and white heads looking over the rim of the nest whenever I leave the house. They're waiting for their parents to come feed them, and it won't be long. Every thirty seconds or so, Mom or Dad returns with a delicious bug to squeals of glee emanating from the nest. This ongoing meal—seemingly all day—is a wonder to behold, the adults so smooth and graceful as they swoop up under the roof, the babies so cute and plainly appreciative, even shivering with pleasure as they receive the morsel of food directly from one beak to another.

While the parents' unfailing feeding schedule is quite impressive, so too is the teamwork of the four chicks on the nest. After the baby at the front of the ledge is given a mouthful, they all rotate one spot to the left, counterclockwise, in unison, so that each one gets its turn every fourth visit. This lovely, gracious, circular ballet continues for hour after hour, day after day, making it possible for the young swallows to grow at a rapid rate.

Normally when the adults were gone, there would be four round heads peeking over the edge, peering down at the monster below. However, if the folks were away for a while—hopefully resting—the little ones would turn inward, their pointed tails sticking outward, as if cuddling, or huddling, perhaps whispering in a secret language no scientist will ever decipher.

Within just nineteen days, the young birds take their first fluttering trial flights. Initially they go but a few feet, from the nest to a nearby window ledge, then a porch beam, and eventually the television antenna on the roof. Meanwhile, their proud parents— and other adults, possibly relatives—are excitedly circling the house and gliding near the new aviators, surely for protection, but also seemingly in exhortation. One can almost hear the grownups cry, "Come on, children, this is how we swallows fly!"

Within two days, the youngsters have graduated from grade school and are taking trips to the backyard clothesline and garden fence, returning off and on to the nest throughout the day and to spend the night. After only three weeks, they have learned to soar like an eagle, dive like a falcon, corner like Steve McQueen in a Corvette, stop in midair like a dragonfly, and hover like a hummingbird, their tiny wings a blur.

Then one morning in early July, I notice the nest is eerily quiet, and the family is gone.

Over the past two years, this particular nest has hosted not only a spring brood of chicks, but a summer batch as well. Within a week or two of abandonment by the first family, the nest attracts another couple and the cycle of fertility begins anew.

Last year, an extra sense of urgency was added to the proceedings. Two young lovers showed up on July 17 and began preparing their home. However, twelve days later, the nest lost its moorings and came crashing down on the stairs! Examining the bird nursery up close, one could not help noticing how exquisitely soft and well lined with feathers the pouch was in expectation of delicate eggs. Surely, no human baby's crib was ever more lovingly padded or tenderly decorated, nor a delivery date more anticipated.

Throughout the day I watched from the window as a number of swallows visited the fallen nest, sometimes sitting together—sadly, it seemed—on the porch railing for several minutes, much like people who come to comfort a neighbor whose house has burned down.

Later that afternoon when I let my cat out the front door, she, of course, discovered the carnage and began sniffing at it. Almost immediately a group of chirping swallows began strafing her like miniature F-16s as if still guarding the nest even though it was now useless (poor kitty didn't stay outside long).

Naturally, I assumed this was the end of the story, at least for the year. However ...

On August 2, just four days after the tragedy, a pair of Barn Swallows began building a new nest in the exact same spot as the old one, returning over and over again with mud, sticks, and straw. In fact, the birds came and went so often I am convinced that the young couple had help from others in their frantic rush to construct a suitable incubator in time for the eggs' arrival. By the next morning, a gray 1½-inch ledge had appeared. On August 4, there was already a three-inch nest with one bird occasionally sitting on it, and by the next evening, the project was finished—a brand-new home in three days!

One week later, the nest was constantly occupied by one or both parents. The babies were born in late August, only three this time, perhaps due to the accelerated schedule. And yet again, thankfully, I was able to witness another family grow and flourish, the chicks take their first tentative flights under the vigilant eye of their elders, and the youngsters eventually join the ranks of the blessed beings who inhabit the sky.

Just four weeks after the chicks were hatched, near the autumn equinox, the swallows left the nest and headed back into the heavens from whence they descended.

The Vallecito Lake Monster

Not long after moving to Vallecito Lake, Colorado, in late 1997, I woke up early one December morning after a series of strange and impossible dreams. Still partially asleep, I walked out on the deck into the stillness and serenity, the half light and half darkness of mountain dawn. It was then, then that I heard the noises for the very first time.

Whoa.

I remember standing there in the cold blue twilight, listening to the eerie, creepy sounds coming from the lake and thinking to myself, "Am I still sleeping and still dreaming? Or is this reality? And if so, how can this thing BE?"

Over the next few weeks I became intimately acquainted with the peculiar, fantastic, highly unlikely, almost unbelievable noises emanating from underneath the steadily growing sheet of ice that was slowly covering the reservoir as it froze up for the winter. After a while, I began to think that the source of these sounds was a mysterious deep-sea creature that had somehow gotten trapped in this high country lake and was trying to escape and return home to the ocean. It was similar to the Loch Ness Monster in Scotland, only this underwater dragon had never been sighted, or photographed, or rarely even noticed by most folks.

Indeed, over time I began to wonder if perhaps only I could hear the exquisitely spooky music, almost haunting in its occasional sadness, almost shocking in its occasional joy. Because, you see, there were a number of mornings when I would stand on my deck overlooking Vallecito, listening in awe to the outrageous symphony, and my neighbors would walk outside to feed the dog or start the car, and never pay any attention to the clearly audible din arising from below. Not once did I witness anyone pause, for even just a few seconds, and savor the bizarre yet lovely noises. The thought entered my head that maybe I was, um, "hearing things." Therefore, not wanting to alarm my new neighbors, just in case I really was "touched," I never mentioned these sounds to anyone the first winter.

In retrospect, it was like being the earliest explorer to ever see the Northern Lights, and then upon returning south to the homeland, wondering if you should tell the others about the rich, sublime, celestial colors that dance in the sky up north.

And so, almost every early morning, while the annual freeze was taking place at the lake, and again for several weeks during spring thaw, I would bundle up good and tight, go outside, and listen. Listen to the noises.

Now, there was such a wide variety of strange and impossible sounds that I hesitate to even attempt to describe them. For, at times, it almost seemed like human voices, or perhaps supernatural ones, singing, humming, groaning, wailing, even laughing out loud! Other times it sounded more like animals howling, barking, and roaring, or birds chirping, whistling, and warbling. There were popping and pinging and dinging and bubbling and burping and snapping and cracking and breaking and tearing noises. There was vibrating and clattering and shattering, booming and thumping and banging. Sounds like .22 caliber gunfire and bullets ricocheting underneath the ice. At times it seemed like submarine sonar or a soundtrack from a scary movie.

Other times, it sounded more like a jet plane taking off, or large boulders rolling down a mountain, or the echo of heavy machinery. Then it would slowly change into a reverberating crescendo of high-pitched noises resonating beneath the ice plate, like dolphins or whales communicating with each other, or perhaps trying to communicate with us land creatures.

And yet, at still other moments, it sounded like a huge, angry sea monster, swimming back and forth, back and forth below the ice. I would get the notion that he was likely, at any moment, to rise up out of the lake and wreak vengeance on the human race for damming Vallecito Creek seventy years ago, thus keeping him from returning to the sea.

And then there were mornings when the curious music exuding from the ice seemed like the very voice of the Cosmos, or Eternity, or Heaven itself, somehow brought to life by water and cold air and sun and sky and contours of the lakeshore and curvature of the planet and movement of millions of molecules in complete coordination. In other words, magic.

Yes, there was something almost divine about the extraordinary racket. Something ethereal, yet earthy. Supernatural, yet tangible. Surreal, yet real. For there were unseen, unknowable forces down there, ever so slowly moving the developing ice around like a conductor moves an orchestra, a master paints a mural, a wizard stirs the pot.

Yet still just another perfectly natural phenomenon, or miracle, or message from the universe. Like seeing a rainbow, or sparrow's breath during winter, or the very first flower of spring. That beautiful, that original, that unexpected, that remembered, that unforgettable THING that makes life so well worth the living.

And so, as December became January, the lake froze as solid as a rock underneath numerous blankets of glittering white snow, and the noises from below were heard no more. However, come spring, the "creature" returned and commenced with his humming, singing, and groaning for another few weeks, before disappearing as the ice melted back into lake water.

Now, I do not know where he goes, or what he does, during the summertime. Maybe the tourists and fishermen and loud motorboats scare him away and drive him down to the very deepest, darkest part of the reservoir where he cannot be disturbed, or seen, or even heard.

But I do know this. Come next November into December, just as the lake begins to ice over for the winter, the splendid monster will return to Vallecito. Yes, one fine, cold, clear morning, along about first light, he'll be back. I guarantee it.

Just as surely as strange and impossible dreams come to us during the night while we sleep.

House of Many Rooms

*Man discovers his deepest self and reveals his greatest creative
power at times when his psychic processes are most free from
immediate involvement with the environment and most under the
control of his indwelling balancing or homeostatic power.*
—Kilton Stewart

What is going on at night?

Just what on earth—or elsewhere—happens to us when we hit
the hay and fall into a deep sleep? What makes our eyeballs bounce
around like a pinball machine behind closed eyelids as if they were
closely watching something vitally important? What causes us to
talk in our sleep, walk in our sleep, and wake up feeling as if we
are living a double life instead of just one? Why do we occasionally
regain consciousness in a cold sweat as if running from the devil
himself, and yet other times awaken in ecstatic bliss as if we had just
visited heaven? And why are so many of us completely oblivious
to the one-third of our existence when we are supposedly "sound
asleep" and yet somehow, some way, fully awake?

For the dream state is not meant to be ignored, avoided, or
swept underneath the rug. Nor is it something to be afraid of. Rather,
we should remain open to the lessons of the nocturnal mind, the
teachings of the unconscious, the learning experiences available
to the unfettered soul as she sails across the cosmos unimpeded
by rules or morals or opinions. We should become aware of, or
perhaps remember, the magic of the night, the light shining in the
sheer blackness, the enlightenment that is attainable in the supposed
darkness.

A primitive tribe in Southeast Asia has developed a fascinating
take on this universal subject. The Senoi people of the Malay
Peninsula believe that the dream state we encounter at night is a sort
of therapeutic trance that allows us to enter a special time and place

wherein our creative forces are free from restraint and thus without normal limits. They consider the time spent sleeping to be a valuable learning tool rather than a puzzling phenomenon, an opportunity for spiritual growth instead of something scary.

Indeed, the Senoi use the waking hour of dawn like a bridge between the two realms. Each morning they gather around the campfire and discuss their dreams, beginning with the youngsters first. From earliest childhood, they are counseled by the elders on how to handle disturbing dreams, see through frightening apparitions, and employ seemingly perilous situations as ways of finding solutions to problems, answers to questions, even access to the divine.

Attackers become teachers. Ferocious animals become helpful friends. The fear of falling becomes the exhilaration of flight. Panic changes to relief. Ignorance evolves into illumination. And darkness transforms itself, as if by magic, into light as certainly as the sun rising above the eastern horizon chases away the night.

Years ago in a dream I discovered a most remarkable place. While walking through deep dark woods by myself I came upon a large clearing with a huge house in the middle. It was white, foursquare, and several stories high. Although the grounds were well manicured and everything seemed in order, the whole area was deathly quiet and apparently deserted. I sensed there was much here for me to explore, to find, to learn about. And how.

I call this building the Mansion of Truth. While I have never actually seen this imposing structure in reality, it is nonetheless real, because I go there almost every night.

When I push open the heavy front door—it is never locked— and walk in, I get the distinct feeling that nobody lives here, it is just a place to visit for a night like a hotel, or all-night movie theater, or amusement park that never closes. Everything is tasteful and elegant, like an old-time Hollywood movie. The sparkling chandeliers, the polished brass, the stained oak, the plush Persian rugs, the overstuffed leather chairs. All is grand and magnificent, yet abandoned and forgotten. Kind of like the dream you had last night that was so impressive when you first woke up, but then it vanished like a ghost, and is now most likely lost forever.

There are many rooms in this house, and just as many mysteries. I walk down long white hallways, opening doors and looking inside. Sometimes I go into a room and spend several hours talking with someone, or watching people behave in peculiar ways, or experimenting with things that are new to me. Some nights I walk through a doorway and suddenly find myself traveling to far-off countries, or riding on a spectral train without an engineer, or flying through the air as if I were a hawk.

Other times I become involved in awkward social situations. I'm attempting to explain something to people who are apparently deaf, or trying to warn society about an impending disaster but no one will believe me, or looking for work in a world of blank-faced automatons, or searching for privacy in a prison where there is none, or moving in super slow motion as if my feet were enveloped in molasses while everybody else is moving at normal speed and staring at me oddly.

And yet there are other nights when I roam the seemingly endless corridors, not opening any doors at all, but rather just enjoying the freedom of choice to not enter any of the rooms.

At the end of the night, as dawn is slowly but surely approaching, I leave the mansion behind and head back through the enchanted forest, always arriving home shortly before waking up in my warm bed with vivid memories which will quickly evaporate into ether if I do not immediately acknowledge them and conduct my own personal private Senoi campfire dream clinic while still half-asleep in a fuzzy trance-like state wherein so much is still possible before the stark reality of morning on planet Earth sets in like fast-drying cement.

Oftentimes at this critical, mystical, magical juncture, I grab my nearby notebook and begin writing down the sublime (or sordid) details of my nocturnal journey as fast as I can. Where I was. Who I was with. What happened.

There are visits—totally unplanned, yet somehow arranged— to mysterious seaports and moonlit cemeteries and deserted Disneylands, sinister train stations and spooky libraries and bizarre apartments, sunny ski areas and stormy beaches and barren wastelands, empty parks and dark factories and alleys full of fog, hospital waiting rooms and high school hallways and silent railroad tracks, Grandpa's farm and Yankee Stadium and a surreal version of San Francisco only vaguely like the real one.

There are visitations from old girlfriends and best buddies and favorite pets, worst enemies and weird strangers and cops asking questions, historical figures and Robinson Crusoe and Elizabeth Taylor, imaginary characters and casual acquaintances and kindergarten playmates not seen in fifty years. There are skid row bums, mountain climbers, dead relatives, friendly waitresses, greasy con artists, phantom hitchhikers, and fantasy lovers.

I find myself involved in blurry baseball games, hypnotic dances, outlandish ceremonies, pre-Christian rituals, close relationships with wild animals, ragged voyages across melancholy America, disoriented wanderings through downtown Vancouver, and dreary all-night-long searches for something that might not even exist. There are circus rides and subterranean tunnels and pirate ships and plants that speak and blue neon lights and red brick walls and Yukon barrooms and boxcars on lonesome sidings and grain elevators out in the middle of nowhere and lots of autumn afternoons for some reason.

There are Twilight Zone episodes playing on my late-night television.

Indeed, anything I could ever remember from my past or imagine in my future is contained within my dream world, plus everything else I *cannot* remember or imagine. From one end of the spectrum to the other, from the heights of heavenly rapture to the darkest depths of despair, from close at hand to oh so far away.

For there are both palaces and dungeons, mountains and valleys, visions and nightmares, uppers and downers, saints and sinners alike in my secret dreamland, my nighttime "other place," my phantasmagoric netherworld where I go while my normal body and normal mind are resting in deep slumber. But I am not.

Because once I fall asleep and let loose of the reins, my unconscious self goes galloping across the landscape like a runaway horse headed for new horizons to behold and new adventures to encounter, before the blaring alarm bell of dawn puts an end to my nocturnal travels for another day. For all kinds of wild and crazy and "impossible" stuff is happening to me as I dream, even while the author of this piece is immobile except for the breathing of his lungs and beating of his heart.

Oh yeah, and the rapid eye movements …

Later on, after awakening from the dream state, I find myself utterly amazed by not only the tremendous differences between the two opposing realities, but also by their shocking similarity. Hopefully, I learn something from the experience. For oftentimes a particular dream at just the right time will "open a door" for me, expose an aspect of my life that needs work, or solve a bewildering predicament that has been bothering me for weeks.

Indeed, dreams are much like windows, or mirrors, or perhaps two-way mirrors that allow us access to the other side of existence. Because these sometimes enjoyable, sometimes painful excursions, viewed in their proper perspective, provide us with invaluable insight into the hidden, secretive, wondrous workings of the universe. These are the sorts of things that are not perceivable in the harsh daylight glare of the waking human consciousness, but rather only while our spirits are set free to roam about wherever they will, wherever they want, real late at night.

Therefore, it is wise to recognize that dreams are much more than merely dreams. Ideally, they become self therapy, catharsis, even enlightenment, all of it available for absolutely free if—and only if—we take the time and make the effort to acknowledge them first thing in the morning before they get away from us like helium balloons disappearing into the sky.

Maybe we modern Americans would do well to follow the lead of the primitive Senoi people and bring our nighttime dreams out into the daylight where they can be examined, analyzed, and appreciated, rather than treating them as if they were unimportant, nonsensical, or even psychotic. For truly there is so very much to be gained from dreams when we open up our real eyes and realize that the Dream Weaver who lives inside the soul is, after all, our friend.

Because oftentimes the darkest things of this realm are the most relevant ones once they are exposed to the light and proven to be not only harmless but surprisingly helpful.

Dream Mesa

There is a hill in my neck of the woods called Bridge Timber Mountain on the 1968 USGS topographical map. However, if you were to ask anyone around here where Bridge Timber Mountain is, they could not tell you. For this hill, or mountain, or whatever, is known to locals by a different name. Actually, a whole bunch of names, mostly with the word "black" in them—Black Ridge, Black Mountain, Black Mesa—because of the dark timber that crowns the summit. The old-timers call it Border Ridge, as it used to be the boundary of the Indian reservation. I myself call it Pink Mesa.

Or Dream Mesa.

Allow me to explain. When I first moved out here in the boondocks it was late November and there was fresh snow on the ground. While watching my first sunset from my new home, everything got real quiet. Unearthly quiet. Then I noticed a white, flat-topped mesa to the east. Only it wasn't really white as in snow white. It was more of a pinkish color, for it was reflecting the colors of the sunset in the southwest. As if it were Alaskan alpenglow, as if it were a huge neon pink rose, as if there were a magical pink light somehow emanating from this mysterious snowy mesa in the sky. So, not knowing its real name, I named it Pink Mesa.

Not long afterward, I got out the maps and found my mesa on the Basin Mountain quad, listed as "Bridge Timber Mountain." This title was probably given to it by the men who logged the tall pine trees that grow on top to build the first bridges crossing the rivers around Durango.

It doesn't fit. So I call it Pink Mesa.

Now, the highest point on Pink Mesa is only 8,366 feet, not lofty by Colorado standards, and especially so since there are 13,000-foot summits only ten miles away. But it is fairly impressive for my neighborhood.

Pink Mesa rises steeply out of dusty old Iron Springs Gulch and is crowned with a flat, forested top. Thus, it is a mesa, not a mountain. The "bench" runs north and south, roughly two miles long by a half-mile wide. It is mostly wooded—aspen, ponderosa, juniper, scrub oak—but there are several open meadows. There are also sacred springs, and secret waterfalls, and wonderful places to spend a day, or a night, or forever.

Not many roads, per se, exist on Pink Mesa, but a few old trails come up from Indian Creek, Sawmill Canyon, and Fortyfour Canyon. No one ever uses them. There is even a village on top. But nobody knows that it is there. Except me. Even though I have never been up there. Because I *have* been up there.

Up there on Pink Mesa. The land where the sun rises. The land where the sunset glows pink on winter snow. The place where dreams come from.

So many dreams. Dreams of Heaven. Dreams of earth. Childhood visions. Memories of angels, and grandmothers, and ravens. Memories of desert journeys and old campsites. Almost forgotten. Never forgotten.

Dreams of a brown-skinned woman … an adobe house … pine trees … velvet purple flowers … flute music … cool water … golden sunshine … hummingbirds and swallows and bald eagles flying through the pearl-blue Colorado sky as if rejoicing.

Visions of ecstasy. Too real to ignore.

For a number of years now I've been dreaming of a place, a place that I have been to before. But I haven't.

This dream place is somewhere in the American Southwest, in between the high mountains and the low desert. It is somewhere between 6,000 and 9,000 feet in elevation. It is in between reality and imagination, in between the here-and-now and what I will dream about tonight while sleeping. And what I dreamt about last night.

As with many of my dreams, I am on the road, roaming around America. At the end of my lengthy travels, I wind up at a friendly little village called Sunny Mesa. It is a warm, peaceful place on top of a plateau somewhere, some hidden, forgotten, enchanted world where the people are all kind to each other and everybody is happy.

Somehow upon arriving I become involved with an outdoor play that the town puts on each summer in the plaza. It seems that everyone has a part in the play, and a place in the life of the village, and no part or place is better than any other.

I get a job fixing things for old folks and painting fences in wild colors. The people accept me as one of their own. I have a genuine feeling of well-being, as if I am finally at the right place at the right time. For I am doing worthy and important work, after all of the other jobs just making money. I have found a beautiful home and feel no need to leave.

Shortly after waking from this dream, these lines appeared in my notebook: "What a magical world this is. Especially if one is not too deeply involved with the logical and techno-logical side of life. For we are magic animals on a magical planet in a magical realm with magic blood flowing through our veins."

For the world I woke up to was not so different from the world that I woke up from …

Indeed, as I looked out the window to the east, the morning sun was rising over Pink Mesa. Over Dream Mesa. Where I had just been.

Where I'm going right now.

Earth Quakies

Most places on this planet experience a distinctive seasonal event that characterizes the heart, the soul, the culture of an area. In the Far North, it occurs when the spring thaw frees the land of snow and ice. In Japan, it happens when the cherry trees blossom and people go to parks to admire the cheerful pink flowers. In baseball cities, it takes place on opening day, in tourist towns at the beginning of tourist season, in fishing villages when the boats come home, in farmland during the harvest, and in ski country when the first snowflakes fly.

Here in the southern Rockies we have our own special period of time that defines our neck of the woods, our way of life, maybe even for some of us the main reason for being here. It arrives each and every autumn, along about late September, like an annual good luck charm from the gods. For this is when the aspen trees turn color.

Coming to southwest Colorado at age seventeen from northeast Nebraska, I felt like an astronaut encountering a previously unknown world. Indeed, there was a brand-new smorgasbord of delights for me to discover, including the extraordinary plant the locals affectionately call "quakie." During my first fall in the mountains, I watched in awe as the sprawling groves of aspen slowly changed from a delicious lime green to a dazzling yellow, even orange and red in spots. It was all so stunningly beautiful that I found it physically impossible to stay indoors on the sunny perfect bluebird afternoons of September and October while the original Artist was painting such a masterpiece.

Since that initial autumn in the San Juans, most of my life has been spent either among the quakies or within a half-hour drive. Whether I am in the Wasatch, Elks, or LaPlatas, the most anticipated time of year is always late summer into early fall, that quintessential state of grace when the aspens put on a show more befitting heaven than earth. There are favorite hillsides, valleys, and even individual groves that must be visited, including one group near my present home that predictably exhibits a shocking shade of hot pink!

I once left Colorado for five years to take care of family. Being six hundred miles from the nearest mountains sorely tested my sanity, especially during the fall. You see, while I missed camping and climbing and skiing the backcountry, wild animals and wild flowers and wild people, rainbows and alpenglow and mornings drenched in diamonds, perhaps what bothered me more than anything was not being able to observe the day-by-day metamorphosis of the aspen leaves from summer green to autumn gold like magic, like alchemy, like a Polaroid photograph gradually developing, like a gorgeous nature goddess gracefully changing garments right before my mortal eyes.

Whoa.

Yes, the "Quaking Aspen" (Latin name Populus tremuloides) is a pretty remarkable tree. Native to North America, its range extends from Mexico all the way to Alaska and across much of Canada, but is most common in the Rocky Mountains. Here in Colorado, aspens prefer sunny south-facing hills as high as 11,000 feet, while their lower-elevation relatives favor the shadier, wetter, north-facing slopes. They are one of the earliest forms of life to emerge from the ground following a forest fire, effectively transforming the charred black landscape into creamy white bark and velvet green leaves within a few short years. This rapid propagation is due to two unusual abilities.

First, each aspen is not an individual specimen, but rather a clone of its neighbors. And each grove of trees is actually just one plant, its roots spreading underground like a secret subterranean strawberry patch network of vines. Saplings pop up here, there, and everywhere, sprouting and reaching for the sky like spring weeds until there is a new forest and no room for more.

Secondly, the quirky quivering quakie possesses quite a knack for accelerated growth. Unlike most trees, its leaves are capable of photosynthesis on both sides. Whether the lustrous green upper face or pale silvery underside is exposed to the sun's rays, its energy is efficiently converted to cell multiplication. The slightest breath of air will cause the thousands of leaves on each tree to tremble and shake, flipping back and forth on their unique four-sided stems, thus affording the entire deciduous surface area access to the life-giving solar radiance emanating from above.

Furthermore, there is something almost supernatural about this rare talent that aspens are endowed with. For when the leaves of a quakie quake, they not only benefit themselves, but also produce a visual display that pleases the human mind in a gentle yet powerful way. Indeed, Native American mothers used to suspend their babies in cradleboards from aspen trees while they were busy picking berries or collecting firewood, for the constant interplay of sunlight, shadow, and movement would keep the papooses entertained and comforted for hours.

Quakies are not only easy on the eyes, but amusing to the ears as well. When the wind blows, they emit a veritable symphony of soothing sounds. At times it reminds me of a softly crackling campfire, stream tinkling over stones, ocean waves foaming on the beach, the whisper of a long-ago lover, or forest faeries singing in celebration of summer.

One of my mentors, Dolores LaChapelle, was particularly fond of aspens. In *Sacred Land, Sacred Sex*, she wrote about being "imprinted on aspen leaves" at an early age. Much like Indian infants of yore, Dolores was put into a canvas seat by her parents and hung from a steel spring hooked onto a tree limb. Thereafter, she was always attracted to quakies, as a pilgrim is drawn to a shrine. In fact, the first place she moved to after finishing college was Aspen, Colorado.

In later years, Dolores would often advise people to "go to the mountains" come autumn. Because if you are lucky enough to live near aspen country you should take full advantage of your good fortune and experience the very finest that nature has to offer, which in her charmed corner of the world was when the changing colors signaled the closing of summer and imminent arrival of winter. For there are few things more enlightening than a leisurely stroll on the sun-dappled floor of an aspen wood while bright yellow leaves cascade all around you with each and every passing breeze.

In essence, Dolores believed that we marvelously gifted human beings should spend our short lives enjoying the splendors of the real, original, created world rather than wasting our precious and irreplaceable time on electronic toys and the unreal, virtual, invented realm. Because, you should understand, we are only given so many—rather, so few—chances to embrace the ultimate on this incredible planet before we die and can no longer do so.

Ever again.

There is an age-old belief (found in several early religions) that Paradise, or Nirvana, or Heaven is actually *here on Earth*, or at least available through various means. I am reminded of this wonderful thought whenever I witness a waterfall in the desert, or falling star just as I look up, or field full of sparkling fresh snowflakes, or flock of geese in V-formation flight, or the reflection of moonlight on lake water.

And yet again each and every autumn when I spot the very first flecks of aspen gold materializing like magic beneath the blazing blue Colorado sky.

The Gray Season

You are lucky, and lucky indeed, if you live where you can fully and deeply experience each of the four seasons. By this I mean all four of them, in all of their beauty, glory, and purity. A real winter, a real spring, a real summer, and most importantly, a genuine autumn. This is important.

I once lived down south—too far down south—and went a whole year without winter. At another time in my life I resided so high up in the mountains that there was precious little summer. In both cases I found myself feeling somehow, somewhat empty inside, as if there were a huge void in my life because I had "missed" one of the four seasons—in more ways than one.

And so, ever since then, I have made sure to live far enough north (but not too far) and at a low enough elevation (but not too low) so as to truly appreciate all four of the sacred seasons, and both passively and actively participate in their comings and goings. Indeed, there are rituals to perform. Traditions to observe. Sights to see, sounds to hear, tomatoes and apples and venison and fudge to eat. These things must be done. Come summer, come fall, come winter, come spring. Come one more time.

However, living here in southwestern Colorado, I have noticed that there are more seasons than just the usual four typically mentioned. There are at least five. Possibly six. What the hay, there may very well be seven or eight different seasons around here. I don't know. But one thing is for certain. There are at least five seasons. For there is, also, the Gray Season.

Now, the Gray Season is the period of time in between autumn and winter when everything suddenly turns gray outside. There seems to be a strange interval, or cosmic pause, that comes just after the spectacular colors and leaves of fall have fallen, and just before the brilliant snows of winter have painted the mountains white. The land becomes gloomy and gray, spectral and mysterious, like an unseen actor changing costumes between acts of a play, or a freight train stopping in the middle of nowhere, or the static on the radio in between stations. In general, an almost unspoken, almost imperceptible grayness envelopes the earth, saturates the scenery, and permeates the air. Everything just turns gray. Plain gray.

The trees turn gray, the bushes turn gray, the sagebrush turns gray, the weeds turn gray. The mountains and hills and mesas turn gray. The pasture, the garden, the woodpile turn gray. Even the very heavens become somber as the clouds of slate and charcoal crowd out the normally neon-blue Colorado sky. Gray, gray, gray. Everywhere gray. But that's okay.

Because I happen to like the color.

Here in the Four Corners region, the gray season, or "fifth season," usually begins in mid- to late October and continues on through most of November, even some years well into December. And while it may appear drab and dreary outside, it is actually a cheerful time of year, at least for some of us. For this is the season of the World Series, of the hunt, of harvest, of Halloween, of my father's birthday, of Thanksgiving, of giving thanks and appreciating blessings. This period, this stretch, this spell, if you will, comes roughly halfway between the Autumn Equinox and Winter Solstice (always two of my favorite days), and foretells the imminent coming of Christmas and the New Year, and even springtime, for without November there would be no May. For one comes only after the other. And then before.

Yes, there is something very special, reassuring, and even comforting about the Gray Season. Comforting like an old gray blanket made of wool. Comforting like a favorite mountain made of granite. Comforting like storm clouds, smoke from a campfire, and roasted meat. Like ashes, and fur, and dirt, and mud, and old wood. Like little gray sparrows, and a cat named Smokey, and the color of Grandma's hair.

For gray is the culmination of all of the other colors, and from whence all colors come. Mix all of the other colors together—red, green, yellow, purple, etc.—and you get gray. Take all the other colors away, and all you have left is gray.

Because, you see, gray is the color of twilight, when secrets are divulged, and mysteries revealed. Indeed, gray was the shade of light to first come out of the night, first to come out of the darkness, first to emanate from the Divine, first to evolve from the Void.

Gray is the first color, and the last color, and therefore the most illuminating of all the colors. Without gray, there would be no other colors, or, at the very least, the other colors would not appear so vivid and bright and pleasurable. Likewise, without the Gray Season there would be no winter of dazzling white, no springtime of emerald green, no summer of rainbows, no autumn of red and gold.

So enjoy, enjoy these gray days of November, this gloomy and surreal time of year in between the colors of fall and the snowfall of winter. Yes, savor, truly savor this grayest of seasons.

While you still can.

Colors of the Cold

January and February. Man, what a drag. Of all the months on the calendar, these two little darlings are always the darkest and dreariest, coldest and creepiest. Kind of like the skeletons we keep locked up in the closet in the hopes that they won't get out. But they always do.

This is the time of year when the poor, pallid sun rises late in the southeast, stays low in the sky all day long, or rather short, and then goes down early—too early—in the southwest. The days are fleeting, the air is frigid, the wind comes howling down from Canada like an angry banshee, and there is nothing you can possibly wear that will keep it from getting inside of your clothing. Nothing.

Now this eerie darkness, this mind-numbing melancholy, this molasses-slow grinding turn of the cosmic wheel always comes just after the warmth and light, the color and cheer of Christmas and the New Year, and well before the first signs of springtime and the return of long and sunny days. Indeed, almost immediately after the Christmas lights are taken down and the holiday decorations put away, there seems to be a sinister cloud of gloom and doom that settles over the land, over the town, and even over the people.

The days get short, the shadows grow long, and the snow piles up in the shade. The ice on the sidewalk never seems to melt, the roads turn slicker than snot, and we drive too fast on them, hurrying, always hurrying to get someplace warm. We bundle up indoors and make excuses to not go outside. We turn on the lights, set the thermostat high, and have the television or stereo playing all the time. In essence, we are avoiding winter, and its attendant darkness and quiet and cold.

But is this the wisest thing to do? Or would it be better to go right straight through the fire, or in this case the bitter chill, the frosty blackness, the very heart of darkness, and come out the other side somehow cleansed and purified? And thus be able to see, with new eyes, the true beauty of this most dismal season of the year.

Because all is not depression, all is not despair, all is not lost. For there are diamonds in the snow, crystals of colored light in the cold air, and even rainbows, of a sort, in the sky. But only if we look.

One time long ago, at the age of nine or ten, I was walking home at night during the middle of winter, in the darkness, alone. It was freezing cold, but I was bundled up good and didn't have far to go. Coming to the last streetlight in town—just before crossing a dark area of trees and railroad tracks to my family's house—I noticed something peculiar. For the light from the lamp up above was illuminating the freshly fallen snowflakes all around me as if they were diamonds and somehow glowing from within. The snow was very light and fluffy and sparkly white, and I was instantly mesmerized by the wonderful silver shimmering little sparkles each and every flake of snow was making and surrounding me with.

This glow, this aura, this cloud of light, this ethereal blizzard of delight enveloping me was holy beyond words and more beautiful than Bethlehem on Christmas morning. My innocent child's mind was bathed, indeed, *submerged* in the sacred silver-blue light that was everywhere, and I suddenly realized that there is no limit to the beauty in this world. That reality, pure and simple reality, can be just as beautiful as we want, if we want, if only we open our real eyes, and see, truly see.

Indeed, if you would like to experience heaven, right down here on earth, I suggest that you go outside, even during the coldest time of year, to fully appreciate the complete and awe-inspiring spectrum of life. For without the cold, warmth would not be such ecstasy. Without darkness and night, there would be no colors and lights. And without winter, there would be no spring of neon green, no summer of wildflowers, no autumn of yellow and orange. Therefore, winter may actually be the most important season of all, and perhaps even the prettiest. Yes, winter.

Winter, with its cooler palette of silvers and grays and blues. People who think the colors of winter are dull and un-inspiring have evidently never left their nice warm houses, or nice warm cars, and walked through the mountains and meadows during January and February. For there is an infinite variety of colors and tints and hues "out there." Indeed, there is no limit.

So get outside this winter, and go for a walk (or snowshoe or cross-country ski) in the deserted woods and enchanted glens.

Check out the special colors that are created by the low angle of the sun, the purity of the air, and the freshness of the canvas. There are white-grays and blue-grays in the snow, dark grays and sable-grays in the shadows, rich Prussian grays in storm clouds and early morning valleys, dull grays on cloudy days, bright grays on sunny days, silver grays on the back-lit edges of snowbanks, and leaden gunmetal grays in the afternoon forest.

But not all is gray in the midwinter mountains, and not all snow is white. Indeed, if the light is just right, and you are lucky, you will witness the legendary "blue snow." Brilliant, stunning, cerulean, almost-sapphire, freaking-too-much BLUE.

When you ski this color of snow, which is normally found only on north-facing slopes above timberline, it feels as if you are actually skiing on the sky. Which is, of course, what you are doing. For this snow, this powder, this miraculous frozen stuff quite literally fell down from the sky. Indeed, from heaven above. And is now on earth.

At dusk, the mountains in winter shed their grays and blues and seem to glow from within with every color of the infinite spectrum. The nature gods and goddesses get out their special paintbrushes and set the visible universe a-shimmering with color, although not so much the bright vivid shades as the subtler yet electric pastels. The pine trees and valleys take on a fuzzy, mystical green aura, the rocky heights become pink and golden with alpenglow, the western horizon changes from scarlet and white to coral and ochre, and the very air molecules become turquoise, lavender, soft violet, purple.

It is as if the snow were holding on to the last colors and last daylight with all its might, yet not fighting the darkness or the coming blue, blue blackness.

I stand on top of a hill in the middle of winter, and watch night arrive in slow motion. All is quiet. All is magic.

All is glowing in the dark.

Waking the Bears

An old Indian legend states that the very first rumbles of thunder heard during early springtime are actually the sounds of grizzly bears waking up after winter hibernation. The huge furry brutes emerge from their dens all grouchy and grumbling and outrageously hungry. It's kind of like when you get up in the morning after skipping supper the day before, and lunch and breakfast, too.

For four months straight.

Naturally, the famished bears begin eating anything and everything in sight, drinking lots of water, stretching stiff limbs and sore muscles, and prowling around searching for signs and smells of family and friends. For there is so much to do now that the gloom and darkness and dormancy of the Long Night is finally over.

Of the four main seasons, spring is always the liveliest and loveliest, the most inspiring and invigorating. This is the time of year when everything is suddenly in motion. The wind, the weather, the climate, the clouds, the streams, the lakes, the ocean tides, the stars and planets and moon all change gears from half-frozen and sluggish to liquid and swift, while the plants, animals, and insects follow suit soon after.

The great migrations begin anew, and commence as they have each spring for a hundred millennia. From snow geese and pelicans and sandhill cranes to antelope and caribou and elk, from sea turtles and sockeye salmon and rainbow trout to ospreys and eagles and buzzards, from wolves and whales and walruses to hummingbirds and butterflies and swallows, the flocks and herds and packs and swarms and schools are on the move. Heading north, as of yore, with the heightening sun, lengthening days, shortening shadows, and warming atmosphere, the animals follow their animal instincts, their natural intuition, their ancient rhythms and schedules, their involuntary, instantaneous, and passionate reaction to hearing "the call of the wild."

Loud and clear.

The brilliant sunshine begins melting the snow, defrosting the ground, and awakening the hills from their cold white slumber. "Spring runoff" (such a wonderful phrase, just the sound of it ignites a fire in my soul) starts in earnest as the creeks and rivers and waterfalls swell and accelerate day by day with the cool clear blood of earth as it makes its way downward, always deliberately downward on its merry way back to the sea. Tiny plants commence popping out everywhere in the undergrowth left over from last year like miniature explosions of green life in a wasteland of tan and gray.

Soon there are weeds growing and wildflowers blooming and buds burgeoning on the bushes and trees. Then comes a warm south wind, the sounds of ducks and crickets and frogs, the scurrying of spiders and lizards and pollywogs, the mating rituals of bugs, the mating dances of birds, the mammal mothers already giving birth. The nests are full, litters large, and a dozen goslings lined up in between their two parents on the pond.

The entire circle and cycle of life seems to automatically quicken in the spring, like an enormous cosmic wheel beginning to spin, or floodgate opening, or boulder suddenly rolling down a mountain. Mother Earth awakens "bright-eyed and bushy-tailed" to the rooster crow of late March, and leaps out of bed raring to go. Every thing still alive after the long icy winter is now atingle with the tremendous potential and endless possibilities of the new dawn, new day, new season, new year now unfolding like the plush velvet petals of an Easter lily.

Yes, when springtime finally arrives in all of her ravishing beauty and resplendent glory, "everything changes," and not just in the natural world. For we human beings feel it also, as our blood thaws and thins and flows a little faster, as we too sense the need to move, to move on, to migrate, to head north, to go somewhere, to do something, to do something so bold and daring and unspeakably wild that we will never forget it.

Indeed, the sights and sounds and smells and tastes and oh-so-powerful feelings that emerge as winter fades away and evolves into springtime remind me of the way a young colt will suddenly race ahead of the herd, kicking his hind heels high in the air all the while. Because when spring fever spreads across the land like a wind-swept wildfire, there is a genuine, irresistible, undeniable spring in the step.

Or should be.

During my late teens and twenties I couldn't wait for spring to come, for that is when I absolutely had to Hit The Road, or else lose my mind. Once the days began to heat up, to brighten, to lengthen, there was no other choice but to go and see the world while I was still young, still crazy, still free enough to do anything I wanted. There was a palpable sense of urgency in the air, for there was so very much that needed to be done. So many places to go, sights to see, and people to meet. Because, as the volcanic, eruptive, explosive month of April approached, it felt like there was "a locomotive in my chest" (Albert Halper) and I could no more sit still than a cougar on the bloody trail of a wounded deer could take a nap.

Indeed, when spring has sprung it is high time to go whole hog or stay home, and I never could stand to stay put, especially once winter is over and done with and the weather changes from cold and dark and dreary to warm, delightful, and ever-so-enticing.

You got to make hay when it's sunny.
—Old farmer saying

Early this winter morning I woke up in the darkness to a deep, low, rumbling sound coming from outside. At first I thought it was just a truck passing by, or somebody showing off the bass range on their car stereo at 3 a.m. However, the noise continued on and off, rising and falling, waxing and waning, with expectant silences followed by gentle booming reverberations. After awhile I began to sleepily realize that the sound was not of human origin, but rather heavenly. For the lovely, dream-like, supernatural music was in fact thunder, good old thunder. The first of the year.

Yes, even though it was still February, normally too early for electrical storms, the soft rumbling, mumbling din moving in from the south was unmistakable. No longer able to sleep, I hopped up, threw on a coat, and headed for the front door. Emerging into the cool night breeze, I felt a tingly chill spread all through my body from more than just one source. For not only was the temperature thirty degrees lower than inside, but the very air molecules seemed to be energized, electrified, and somehow alive. Looking up I saw no stars or moon at all, but rather the reflection of the town streetlights gently bouncing off the low-hanging cloud cover that had moved in overnight. Then, all of a sudden, there it was.

Lightning.

Not an actual instant vividly bright bolt of white-hot molten lava streaking down from sky to earth, but lightning nonetheless, as a soft luminescent glow ricocheted from cloud to cloud. Then slowly, slowly but surely, came the comforting, primeval, ever-so-familiar noise I had heard earlier while lying in bed, only this time in full harmonic stereo.

Ooohh.

No longer chilled, I sat down on the front porch and enjoyed the show. Here it comes again. I began counting the time lapse in between the flash of light and roar of distant thunder. Twenty seconds, then fifteen, then ten. Getting closer, brighter, gradually louder and louder, as if someone were slowly turning up the volume on a celestial boombox.

When the thunder sound was about five seconds away, and thus the lightning a mile off, the first drops of sky water started falling pitter-pat on the sidewalk, and we received our initial rainstorm of the spring even though it was still officially winter. Now fully, utterly, hopelessly awake, I gave up on getting any more sleep and decided to spend the rest of the night watching the lightning, listening to the rain, and marveling at the booming, banging, thundering racket emanating from above. For the annual miracle had now begun.

Centuries ago in northern Europe, the Vikings believed that the fantastic noises produced by lightning storms were actually the sounds of their beloved thunder god Thor flying through the clouds and playing drums with his mighty hammer Mjöllnir. Later on, of course, came the know-it-alls with their scientific explanations and meteorological theories about negative ions, colliding air masses, electrical discharges, blah blah blah. But I'm not buying it. Why not? Because, you see, I prefer a little bit of magic with my Mother Nature, especially when it comes to the most awe-inspiring events in the entire universe. Things like rainbows and tornadoes and volcanoes, earthquakes and northern lights and meteor showers, full moons and ocean tides and massive migrations of animals.

Yes, I tend to believe the old legends concerning thunder, whether they be a Nordic deity doing a drum solo in the clouds, a band of angels playing music in the heavens, angry gods fighting it out with bolts of lightning, or even grouchy old grizzly bears grumbling loudly as they emerge from their winter dens at the very first sign of spring.

For there is something profoundly rejuvenating about the flash of lightning and crack of thunder coming down upon us from up above. It's almost as if the cosmos is encouraging us to WAKE UP and truly savor this most precious season of them all, while also advising us to now decide what we really need to do this year, this go-around, this dance, this chance, this time to make hay. Just in case it is our last one.

Therefore, be sure and pay close attention to what the spring thunder is saying to you, because there is so much to be done in this life, for hungry bears and human beings alike.

Now that we are both awake.

The Little Girl Who Loved Lilacs

We all go to Heaven leaning on the arm of someone we helped.
—Neal Cassady

The power and majesty and beauty of Nature are oh-so-obvious during an avalanche, or thunderstorm, or sunset on the ocean. But sometimes it is the smaller, subtler things of the Universe that touch us in our very innermost soul … like the smell of lilacs in spring.

While living in Salt Lake City, I dated a girl named Becky, whose mission in life at that time was to take care of an elderly woman named Alta. Now, Alta was over ninety years old, and weighed less than ninety pounds, but she had a good mind, a lovely smile, and a genuine twinkle in her eye.

Her family, however, did not appreciate her special kind of beauty, and indeed seemed to be waiting for her to die so they could divide her money and possessions. They left her in that apartment for days and weeks on end, so whenever I would go over to see Becky we would put Alta in her "race car" (wheelchair) and take her for a "ride" around the neighborhood. She truly reveled in these walks, and Becky told me that she looked forward to my visits more than the rare occasions when her son or daughter or grandchildren would come by.

"You better be nice to Curt," she would tell Becky. "He's the only one besides you who takes me outside."

And Alta loved outside.

It was springtime in Utah, and Becky and I were pushing Alta along a quiet little street when we passed a church. I heard old Alta moan in a high voice.

"What's the matter?" I asked.

"Oh, look at the lilac blossoms!" she cried. On the other side of a chain-link fence was a row of healthy lilac bushes in full bloom. Their fragrance was sweet and heavenly.

"Oh, I wish I could have a flower," she said in a soft voice. Alta rarely asked for anything, but she really wanted this.

"No problem," I said, and climbed over the fence. I broke off several small branches loaded with lavender blossoms, and returned.

Walking up to Alta to give her the flowers, I saw her ancient eyes grow tender and young. She suddenly looked like a little girl on Christmas morning.

When I handed her the blossoms, her face seemed to say, "Oh, I am not worthy." But she ever-so-slowly accepted the gift from my hands, and gently brought the lilac flowers up to her nose.

I will never forget the noise she made as she sniffed them. It was a cross between a shiver that gives you goose pimples and a groan of sheer ecstasy. Becky and I watched Alta in awed silence as she hugged the lilacs to her bosom. She seemed to be glowing, as if there were light coming out of her.

When we got home, we put Alta in her favorite chair and placed the lilac blossoms in two vases, one on either side of her. Becky told me later she'd never seen her look happier.

This was Alta's last spring on earth. Her family sent her to southern California for "health reasons," far from the mountain valley where she had lived her entire life. She died soon after.

There are things in this world that we should best forget, and there are things in this world we should never forget.

And so it is that each year, when the month of May rolls around, when the snow has left the valley and moved back up into the mountains, and the land is green and growing once again, and I smell the first lilac blossoms of spring, I think of Alta, the little old lady I met years ago. I think of Alta, the beautiful little girl who loved lilacs.

And always will.

Teacher in a Wheelchair

A few years of trouble, ten thousand years of bliss.
—Chinese proverb

Hobbling across the parking lot like a crippled old man, I was feeling mighty sorry for myself. My injured back was not getting any better, and I had begun to wonder if the constant nagging pain would ever go away. The doctors and surgeons, specialists and therapists, chiropractors and acupuncturists, pain pills and cortisone injections, spinal manipulation and electrical stimulation did not seem to help me, and my insurance coverage and savings account were both running out. Therefore, I was being "shown the door" and left to battle the problem alone.

Such was my mindset as I entered the grocery store in Durango, Colorado, that afternoon to pick up a few things on my way home. Walking down the aisle, I spotted a young man in a motorized wheelchair. His entire body was twisted and deformed. Something horrible had happened to him, possibly while still in the womb, and as a result his arms and legs and torso and neck were all curled around each other in a hideously disfigured distortion of what we normally consider to be the human body. Indeed, everything was completely out of whack.

Well, not quite everything …

For right behind the boy stood his mother, a small blonde woman with a round and gentle face. Blissfully shopping for groceries while simultaneously operating the control stick at the rear of the wheelchair, she seemed to be moving in some sort of sacred synchronicity with her son as if they were one living being rather than two.

I could see the whole story with just that first look. The early signs of trouble, the worry, the diagnosis, the confirmation. The silent agony, the growing darkness, the "Why me, Lord?" questions.

The endless doctor appointments, the operations, the ever-ongoing therapy. And yet also plainly apparent was that stubborn, steely, never-say-die attitude so conspicuous in human beings when they are cornered.

Because, you see, that child needed help, lots and lots of help, and his mother gave it to him. Simply, freely, unconditionally. In essence, his suffering became hers, and her joy became his. Something was being shared here, exchanged here, transformed here. It reminded me of a scene in the movie *Resurrection* where the healer cures a crippled woman of a similar affliction, but then temporarily exhibits a grotesque contortion of her own limbs, even as the patient stands up for the first time in her life.

This marvelous little film from 1980 starring Ellen Burstyn is based on a true story about a woman who almost dies in a car crash, but then somehow returns from Heaven with the ability to lay hands on sick people and heal them. When pressed to reveal exactly which God or entity enables her to perform such miracles, she describes it simply as "the power of love."

As I neared the woman and her son in the wheelchair at the end of the supermarket aisle, he appeared to be trying to say something, but it wasn't easy for him to do. His mother leaned down to listen, and then suddenly both of them burst out laughing! Whatever he said was obviously outrageously funny, and the two of them enjoyed a good long belly laugh together.

Normal, healthy, able-bodied people walking past must have wondered what these poor souls could possibly have to laugh about, and yet laugh they did. Unrestrained, unashamed, unstoppable mirth emanated from them both like repeated ocean waves splashing upon the shore, as if they had not a single care in the world.

Instead of a hundred of them.

As I passed this tender scene, my mind began to run down a list of things that the young man had never done, and probably never would do, and yet he seemed, at least for a precious minute, to be as happy as a spring meadowlark. For he would most likely never stand up on his own, or dress himself, or use the bathroom alone, or take a shower without assistance. He would never walk to school, play on a playground with the other kids, ride a bicycle, or learn how to throw a spiral pass with a football. He would never go hunting with his dad, drive a car, dance with his girlfriend, plant a garden, build a garage, or get a good job. He would never experience the delights of camping out in the desert, the sensuous thrills of skiing powder, the fluid exhilaration of surfing, the adrenaline rush of whitewater rafting, or the sheer physical and spiritual satisfaction of climbing a high mountain.

He would never make it to Alaska.

The list went on and on in my head, but to further describe it would only depress both reader and writer. Suffice it to say, I suddenly found myself in a totally different frame of mind than the pitiful one I'd known only minutes earlier. For as I walked around the store—on my own two legs—and carried my groceries—with my own two hands—and prepared to leave—all on my own—I stopped moping and feeling sorry for myself. My back problem no longer seemed so serious, so worrisome, so capable of ruining my entire life. In fact—almost miraculously—I could scarcely feel it anymore.

Just before heading out the door, I glanced back and saw the young man in the motorized wheelchair approaching the checkout stand with Mom right behind him. Although no longer laughing out loud, both were wearing serene looks on their faces in spite of the enormous lifelong affliction that they shared. For the two of them, together, had discovered the key to happiness.

While I was still learning.

The Can Lady

I have a good friend named Shirley who collects aluminum cans. She shuffles around the neighborhood dressed in her tan baseball cap, black jacket, and pink sweatpants looking for treasures to put in her plastic grocery bags. Although mentally handicapped, and somewhat limited in her vocabulary, she is not lacking in the social skills. For Shirley is a very nice person, and has lots and lots of buddies around here.

And hopefully no more meanies.

I first met Shirley shortly after moving to town. We hit it off right away, and indeed have several things in common. One of them is walking alleys. She's looking for cans to sell to the recycler, and I am searching for things to write about. We usually meet once or twice a month on our journeys of discovery, and always have time for a little chat.

When I asked her what her name was, she tried to tell me, but had trouble pronouncing the word. So she pulled out her pen and notebook and spelled it on paper for me in large capital letters: "S-H-I-R." Then, when she came to the end of the page and ran out of space to write, she shifted gears and headed down the right margin in much smaller letters: "l-e-y."

"Shirley!" I said. "That's a pretty name."

She almost blushed. "Thank yoooo."

Now Shirley's voice may be slow and slurred and sometimes difficult to understand, but her eyes are straight and honest, her smile pure and bright, her spirit still intact in spite of her obvious limitations. Her speech pattern is a partly sorrowful, partly hopeful, partly comical mixture of Minnie Pearl and John Wayne in slow motion, and our conversations are always conducted at roughly one-half the speed that normal reality moves at.

While making her weekly rounds, Shirley greets everyone she meets with a cheerful "Helloooo," and leaves them with a melodic "Bye-bye." She talks with the old folks and young folks alike. She communicates with the little kids and the cats and the dogs. Even the ones who bark at her repeatedly receive a warmhearted "Hi puppeeee" from Shirley. For Shirley is a living angel.

Neighbors tell me "the can lady" used to stay with her parents until they both died a few years back, and then moved in with her brother down on 8th Street. She cannot hold a regular job, so she collects cans and sells them for "cash money." Several days a week, she walks the streets and avenues and alleyways in pursuit of aluminum. And she does pretty good at it too, mainly because so many people on the south side save their cans for Shirley and put them out for her to pick up once a week (she hits my place every Monday morning at about 9 o'clock).

Not only that, but I have noticed that the local garbagemen—big burly bearded guys who melt into instant cupcakes at the sight of a handicapped woman trying to make a couple of bucks—go through the trash and toss the empty cans on the ground for her to find. She knows their schedule, and vice versa, and oftentimes follows them up and down the alleys on weekday mornings, jabbering away in a lilting slow-motion singsong sort of voice. Indeed, the people around here are so kind to Shirley she occasionally has trouble carrying all of the cans home! I see her trying to coordinate holding onto six or seven yellow and white plastic bags bulging with aluminum gold as she makes her way along the sidewalk, doing what the can lady can.

Shirley likes to sort and count the cans she acquires and then write down the results in her notebook. One day by the old grade school she said to me, "You had 25 beer cans and 4 pop cans last week." I told her, "Well, just don't tell anybody about the pop cans."

Her face lit up like fireworks on the Fourth of July.

And so you see that Shirley not only provides a necessary service as the neighborhood aluminum recycler, but she also gives, receives, and appreciates the simple things, the human things, the heavenly things of this world. Things like conversation and humor, good health and fine weather, warm sunshine on a cold morning and cool shade on a hot afternoon. Caring and sharing. Gifts being passed from one hand, one voice, one pair of eyes to another. The stuff that makes life so worth the living.

However, sorry to say, not everyone on Shirley's route is so pleasant. One time, with a painful expression on her hopelessly innocent face, she told me about a mean old man named Bobby who yelled at her for getting into his trash, and even called her "bad words."

I tried to comfort her by saying, "Well, there are some bad people in this world, but most folks are pretty good. He probably can't help it."

"No," she sadly agreed, "he can't help it."

Then, just recently, she informed me that "Bobby won't bother me no more." When I asked her why, she replied, "He die."

As she slowly spoke these two short words, her voice cracked and changed from joyful relief to inward sorrow as she—and I—suddenly realized that the mean old man had died and left this world forever without ever learning how to be nice to people.

Lesson number one.

The heartbreaking way in which she related this story made me see that Shirley is very much a little child inside, and there is nothing wrong with that. Indeed, sometimes while talking with her, I get the distinct feeling that I also am still somewhat of a child, and it is not necessarily a coming down to her level, but rather perhaps a re-awakening within me of the real essence of living well, that is, one moment, one aluminum can, one alley, one morning, one blessed day at a time.

For there are lessons to be learned from people like Shirley. Lessons of kindness, humanity, and humility. Teachings on the ability to put forth our very best effort in spite of our disabilities. Be they great or small.

One time during an early morning conversation, Shirley said to me, "You a nice guy."

I told her, "Why, thank you. You're a nice lady."

Then, as I was walking home and feeling pretty good about the upcoming day, I thought to myself, "I sure am glad there are so many nice people in this world, and so few mean ones."

If only for Shirley's sake.

The Only Hippie in the Oklahoma Panhandle

Sometimes the best way to learn about people is to be the opposite of them. Occasionally the most enlightening lessons of all are those that seem the most unlikely. And every once in awhile, the very last place on earth you think you want to be is actually the first.

October 1975. On the road. Outskirts of Liberal, Kansas. I had just hopped a freight train from Dalhart, Texas, across the Oklahoma panhandle to southern Kansas and was hitchhiking north to Nebraska. Nearing the end of my initial journey around western North America, it was now tree-turning, day-shortening, night-chilling autumn, and therefore time to find a place to spend the winter before the magical mystery tour commenced anew the following spring. Having just turned nineteen, I was savoring a genuine joyride with life, and couldn't wait to do whatever was next on my "list of things to do before I die." That's when I met Gorey Waugh.

Yes, Gorey Waugh.

Thumbing on highway 54 at the edge of town, I noticed the shiny white work truck headed my way and figured it would stop. Sure enough, the guy slowed down and pulled over. I threw my pack in back and climbed into the cab. He was an irrigation engine mechanic from Guymon, Oklahoma, who was just starting his own business. We hit it off right away, in spite of the fact that he was a buzz-cut cowboy and I was a longhaired hippie. Gorey was driving 70 miles northeast to Cimarron, Kansas, to pick up some parts and see some people. Although perfect strangers, we began telling each other outrageous tales from our travels and laughing our heads off like a couple of little kids left alone in a sandbox. He bought me lunch at a truck stop in Meade where the food was as fine as Grandma's kitchen and the conversation just as pleasant. We stopped at a couple other places along the way, and it seemed that everybody not only knew Gorey but also dearly enjoyed teasing him (a sure sign of respect in the country). Before letting me off at the north end of Cimarron, he offered me a job with his new company, even though I admittedly knew very little about engines. I told him I might be back after visiting Nebraska.

Later on it was learned that a number of local gearheads badly wanted to work for Gorey. So why he hired me as his first and only employee straight out of the blue shall forever remain a secret. Perhaps I happened to be at the right place at the right time.

And so it was that I returned eleven days later to the town of Guymon (this time in a car instead of a boxcar), which sets right smack-dab in the center of the Oklahoma panhandle, the long slender strip of desolate windswept prairie jutting out from the northern left corner of Oklahoma proper like a gigantic fateful finger pointing west, go west, young man. Even though knowing only one person there—a guy who picked me up hitchhiking—I felt confident in my decision to conduct a unique experiment. In other words, I wanted to learn about the unknown, the unusual, the unpredictable. Because there is nothing like fresh blood to liven things up ...

I should mention that while in my late teens I looked like a member of the musical *Hair* with a curly, uncontrollable, sun-bleached blond mop on top of my head that hung down past my shoulders and went sideways just as far. So moving to a part of the world inhabited by clean-cut, straight-laced, bible-thumping rednecks only made it stand out all the more. Yes, my "freak flag" was definitely flying proudly, loudly, majestically in the breeze for all to see, and I never once considered cutting it to please the local crowd. Why not? Partly because I like long hair, partly because I enjoy being different from the herd, but mainly because I'm just plain ornery.

Therefore, other than for Gorey and his family and circle of friends, I was not exactly welcomed with open arms by the good people of Guymon. Not only was I a Stranger in Town, but a longhaired one to boot. Indeed, some of the initial looks I received that first day, first week, first month could have frozen a camera shutter shut. Rarely before or since have I seen or sensed such instant suspicion, such quickly slitted eyes, such unconcealed hatred at my mere presence. It was almost as if I were suddenly a red or brown or black person instead of a white one, as if I were a foreigner in an unfriendly land rather than an American in America, as if I were immediately branded a sinner by a thousand canonized saints.

This behavior, mind you, came from a group of folks who almost universally worship—at least on Sunday morning—a God whose only begotten Son not only wore long hair and a beard, but sandals and a dress-like robe as well! Go figure.

Being the sole hippie in a county full of cowboys and cowgirls, I began to find out a few facts about my new neighbors in particular and the human race in general. As a "minority" for the first time in my life, I determined from people's peculiar reaction to my God-given hair that the roots of prejudice sprout from the fertile soil of ignorance and fear, and furthermore to judge a person by his looks, skin color, choice of religion, country of origin, or length of hair makes as much sense as throwing away a good book because you dislike the front cover.

While I did encounter unpleasant attitudes toward my golden locks of unruly fur, my saving grace was being "Gorey's buddy." For I soon discovered that Gorey Waugh was the most beloved man in the entire town, and thus the vast majority of folks would not dare step on his toes by hassling me over my hair. Oh, occasionally somebody would make a remark—something brilliant like "Is that a boy or a girl?"—but usually when I was outnumbered ten to one by tough guys who would never be outnumbered because they would never leave home. Which told me all I needed to know.

So there I was in Oklahoma with a new job, new life, new turn of the page. Initially I rented a dingy room at the decrepit Alexander House hotel for $15 a week with degenerates loitering in the lobby and mice running up and down the hallways like they owned the building. But then a small cabin out back became available for $25, and I merrily moved in with my few meager possessions. It was the only place I had ever lived at by myself, and it became home, sweet home, be it ever so humble, for the next six months. And what a six months it was.

Not only was I living alone for the very first time, but was, essentially, ALONE for the first time. All of a sudden I had no pals my age, no girlfriend, no nearby family, no social structure whatsoever like I had known back home, and then again in Colorado where I had spent the previous winter. But rather than becoming lonely, desperate for love, or longing to fit in with the Guymon scene, I instead used this singular opportunity to learn about myself.

And other important things.

Indeed, I did not feel left out or alienated during my self-imposed exile, but rather reveled in being alone, in being a loner, in flying solo for a change. I discovered many wonderful new—and old—activities that are rarely ever experienced when one is among people, or while being watched. For the universe and its endless list of miracles is most honestly perceived through one's own eyes and no one else's.

And so, with a social calendar that was almost always blank, I had lots of free time after work and on weekends to take off on personal voyages of discovery not unlike those of the great explorers. For there is so very much quality, quantity, and variety available in this world if only we are not too busy to venture out, look for, and find it.

For instance, I would go on long meandering drives in the country in my '67 Plymouth Fury with no map or direction or destination in mind, trusting my instincts at each intersection, and see which neighboring state I came to. Choosing a totally different return route to Guymon, I would pick up every hitchhiker on the road and take them wherever they wanted (my way of showing gratitude for the many kind souls who picked me up the previous summer). I would cruise up to Liberal on a regular basis for the pretty girls, the legal Kansas beer, and the only decent bookstore in a hundred miles.

I spent the Christmas holiday down in Amarillo, Texas, walking the streets and starting conversations with total strangers I'd never see again. I went for peaceful hikes along Beaver Creek in the winter sun, and never saw another person even though it was the only public land around. I went for blissful saunters during the rare rainstorms when everybody else would hide inside their houses. And I went for Sunday morning strolls through deserted downtown Guymon like something from out of a Johnny Cash song.

It was at this point in my early development that I became the "Midnight Rooftop Rambler" (based on the lyrics of an old Rolling Stones tune) whereby I would climb on top of the buildings overlooking Main Street on Saturday night and prowl around like a cat burglar. And yet occasionally I could no longer contain my immense excitement and would howl out loud in a high-pitched voice like a demented coyote, practically daring someone to call the cops (which nobody ever did).

I learned something about children during this phase: they like to look up. While grownups normally keep their eyes focused at street/sidewalk/storefront level while cruising downtown, the little boys and girls riding in the backseat of the family Chevrolet would oftentimes be staring upward at the signs and streetlights and skylines of buildings. In fact, the only people who ever witnessed my nocturnal escapades were kids who spotted me peering over the edge from three stories high while watching the traffic below. The whites of their eyeballs would literally enlarge as they saw me.

One can only imagine the priceless dialogues that took place in the passing automobiles. "Daddy, Daddy, there's a longhaired hippie like on television running around on top of the movie theater!" Of course, by the time Dad slowed down and looked, I would have disappeared into the darkness like The Shadow. "Sure, Tommy, sure. Right here in Guymon, Oklahoma. Were Batman and Robin with him? No more soda pop for you tonight, young man!"

I bought a basketball and played games by myself at the only court in town because nobody else ever showed up. I went to movies all alone for the first time in my life. I sat in the empty park and watched the ducks paddle around the pond. I hung out at the cemetery.

However, while enjoying plenty of splendid solitude, I did not shy away from society. One day I went to a livestock auction at the sales barn with Gorey and his wife where stern-faced cowboys stared at me until I stared right back. I attended a rodeo outside of Goodwell, Oklahoma, where I was about as inconspicuous as a circus clown at a funeral, a wolf walking nonchalantly into the Westminster dog show, or a black sheep with pink polka dots among a flock of pure white ones. Somehow, I was invited to Thanksgiving dinner at the mansion of the wealthiest family in town, but came away more revolted by their inflated egos and perverted interpretation of Christianity than impressed with their numerous possessions and lofty standing in the community.

I fell in love with a Mexican girl I met at church and just as quickly fell out. I got into strange discussions with lonely housewives at the local laundromat. I found myself talking with truck-stop waitresses, old men in coffee shops, migrant workers, born losers, and seemingly boring folks whom nobody else would talk with. I discovered that there is more than meets the eye to people who are not pretty, popular, or privileged.

At my new line of work I learned how to overhaul huge gasoline irrigation engines (534 cubic inch Fords, 549 Internationals, 702 GMC's) and then take them out to the fields to feed the thirsty crops. I became fond of country music, the mooing of cattle, and wide-open spaces with endless panoramas. I loved watching the pastel colors of morning metamorphosing in the clouds, the vivid orange and scarlet hues of sunset on the prairie radiating like a neon bonfire across the sky, and the luminescent glowing of the full moon as viewed from the exact middle of nowhere.

I finished my study of the Bible and began my exploration of the Tao Te Ching. I read powerful, eye-opening, life-changing books by Muir, Steinbeck, and Kahlil Gibran. I devoured Kerouac's *On the Road* for the second time in several months while fantasizing about my next trip the coming spring. I conducted mind-blowing experiments with "train of consciousness" writing. I kept a dream log of my nighttime adventures while asleep. I composed zany, cryptic, mystical poems which did not make any sense until many years later.

There was a re-awakening of my long-dormant penchant for drawing. I started carrying my notebook with me and sketching whatever caught my eye or came into my head. There are pictures of a rodeo arena lined with cowboys who all look alike, a log cabin in the wilderness overgrown with vegetation, the abandoned Buffalo schoolhouse east of town, a customized dual-carburetor V-12 monster of a motor I built at the shop, and my kitchen table with a cigarette smoking in the ashtray.

There are portraits of an Indian chief standing in a patch of maize, a bearded sea god saving a drowning baby, The Man With No Name holding a menacing six-shooter, a guy with a floppy hat flying down the highway toward the mountains, and my alter ego "Odysseus America" sailing through the cosmos on wings of rainbow-colored feathers. There's a map of the western half of the North American continent with my summer of '75 travels outlined in red ink, a drawing of my car leaving Guymon in a cloud of dust, and a self-portrait of me staring into the mirror like a curious ape-man.

Indeed, contained within my early "road journals" is evidence of a young man investigating the raw essence of life, opening brand-new doors, and asking age-old questions. Certainly, there are signs of an adventurous soul on a serious search for the pure something, the holy whatever, even Heaven itself. And truly, there is tangible proof of the unexpected benefits to be gained from spending six months in semi-isolation. For little by little, day by day, week by week, I slowly but surely came to the stunning, electrifying, supremely liberating realization that to be happy in this realm you not only have to *be* yourself, but *please* yourself.

Because, you see, nobody else can do that.

In fact, in truth, in sheer ecstasy I did a whole bunch of beautiful things that winter in Oklahoma that I'd never done before, may never do again, and surely would not have discovered if I had caved in, conformed, cut my hair, and became a part of the crowd. For there was special stuff I had to do, certain people I was supposed to meet, and several lessons I needed to learn before moving on to the next chapter in my novel, one-of-a-kind, spine-tingling, page-turning, ever-ongoing book.

Oh yeah, I almost forgot. I also entered a Golden Gloves boxing tournament on a "wild hair" and wound up winning the heavyweight trophy by defeating a crew-cut cowboy from Kansas on a last-round knockout in front of a full house at the county fairgrounds.

I'll bet you his buddies teased him about losing to a girl.

Epiphany on Grand Mesa

Lying there in my sopping-wet sleeping bag in the middle of the night in the midst of a monster once-in-a-lifetime lightning barrage, I realized that I had strayed too close to the razor's edge.

For the final time.

What the hell was I thinking, or rather, *not* thinking while making the ill-fated decision to camp at the westernmost point of the towering mesa? Surely I must have noticed how high, how close to the sky, how exposed, how vulnerable it was to summertime storms. Surely I must have recognized that this distinctly beautiful place was also an obvious magnet for electrical strikes. And certainly I had to have been completely out of my bloody bleeping mind to stay there anyway. But now it was too late, way too late, and the wicked bolts of lightning were zapping the ground all around me like a tap-dancing pyromaniac with only a cheap leaky tent in between myself and instant incineration.

Yes, once again my love of spectacular views had superseded my better judgment and put me directly in harm's way. Indeed, if brains were money I'd be flat broke.

Earlier that afternoon I had been leisurely driving across the top of Grand Mesa in my old black pickup truck, headed west, bound for the far edge of the vast wooded plateau to a place appropriately known as "Land's End." As luck (both bad and good) would have it, I had the summer off from the rat race and was therefore exploring a wide variety of wild places in western Colorado and eastern Utah. Lots of high mountains and low deserts, red rivers and blue reservoirs, deep canyons and enchanted mesas. And now came the biggest mesa of them all, the Grand. Having seen this geological monstrosity from every possible angle over the past twenty years, I figured the viewpoint at the very western end must surely be one of the most stupendous of them all.

And how.

Being a veteran climber, experienced camper, and lifelong weather watcher, I naturally know the Rocky Mountains' penchant for thunder clouds popping up out of nowhere on a daily basis during the warmest months of July and August. However, these quick and violent storms are normally just afternoon events, and gone by evening. So, while bouncing along on washboarded National Forest roads, I kept one eye on the scenery and one eye on the sky, the deep blue turquoise Colorado sky. If it stayed clear, I hoped to camp near the cliffs at 10,000 feet and enjoy the complete light show including sunset, moonrise, stars appearing, and the Milky Way galaxy sailing serenely across the universe, all while overlooking a good portion of "my little corner of the world."

Upon finally reaching the end of the road, end of the mesa, end of the world itself it seemed, I was treated to quite a sight. After fifty miles of driving through dense coniferous forest, suddenly everything opened up to an entirely different scenario, like a pair of curtains parting as the lights come on and the performance begins.

Whoa.

Before even parking, I knew I had found heaven on earth. For spread out below, above, and all around was a delectable feast for hungry eyes. The 360-degree panorama, shimmering in the heat waves of summer, included the West Elks, Chinese Mountains, and San Miguel range in the south; the Grand River Valley, Uncompahgre Plateau, and La Sals over in Utah to the west; the Roan Cliffs, Palisade Peak, and Debeque Canyon to the north; the Flat Tops, Anvil Point, and Piceance Basin in the faraway northeast; and the huge evergreen humpback of Grand Mesa hovering on the eastern horizon like a grizzly bear about to awaken.

As my long-range vision roamed from one familiar landmark to another, I also noticed a small patch of dark clouds clear off on the southwestern skyline, but it did not seem threatening. Not at the moment.

After setting up the tent, collecting firewood, and organizing camp, I went for a walk along the edge of the gorgeous abyss. Overlooking the golden green immensity of western Colorado was like viewing the miracle of ongoing creation, and I marveled at being so blessed to be present at this particular curl of the eternally curling wave.

Following supper cooked over an open fire, I went out to the farthest, highest, most vertical cliff and prepared to watch the ceremony. As the earth of daylight rotated like an enormous celestial wheel into the night of earth, I witnessed a magnificent orange-flaming sunset ever so slowly metamorphose into a dark rich cobalt sky dotted with stars shining like a thousand miniature suns.

There would be no moonrise.

As I buttoned down camp for the night and prepared to hit the hay, the wind came up and smelled of rain. Not a good sign. Then I noticed that the stars in the southern sky were quickly disappearing, much like the fire being put out in the pit.

Upon entering the tent, I zipped the door shut and crawled into my sleeping bag. I lay in the darkness and considered the possibility of an approaching storm. Hopefully there would be just a little wind, maybe some rain, perhaps a bit of lightning on the higher terrain, then the clouds would move along to the east before colliding with the 14,000-feet Elk Range. I drifted off to sleep.

Then, a couple of hours later, all hell broke loose.

I awoke to the sound of an explosion nearby. "Man, that was close," I said to myself. The next one was right on top of me.

Having survived several close brushes with death by electrocution over the course of a hundred summit ascents (and attempts aborted by storms) I was intimately familiar with the sizzling noise that lightning makes at high elevation a split second before it strikes. Instinctively shutting my eyes tight, I witnessed the awe-inspiring sight nonetheless, for the mighty flash of pure unadulterated light entered my retinas as if tent canvas and human eyelids did not exist.

After immediately uttering a few choice cuss words (if only to acknowledge being alive) I began lecturing myself for being such a damn fool greenhorn to camp on the very tip of a lightning rod in the middle of July! How could I have *done* such an idiotic thing? But there was nothing to do now except ride it out.

While listening to the crack and boom and roar of the constant thunder, I could feel the ground below me shake in unison. All was movement, sound, and fury. There was a powerful wind out of the south, incessant pounding rain, and bolts of sheer, primal, supreme energy frying treetops and high points of wet rock all around my forlorn campsite. The borrowed bargain-basement tent posing as "shelter" was bending and groaning in the tempest like a branch about to break, flapping like a bedsheet on a Wyoming clothesline, and springing leaks faster than a cheap rubber raft in shallow rapids.

After awhile it felt like I was living in a house with half the roof and most of the walls gone. Becoming increasingly concerned about the puddles of highly conductive rainwater rapidly forming on the floor, I kept moving my sleeping bag from one dry spot to another until there were no more left. Then I just huddled in the absolute wetness of it all and hoped for the best.

Being right in the center of the electrical storm, I felt as helpless as a rowboat in a hurricane. Having no say whatsoever in whether I lived or died that night, I realized with a fright that my very survival was entirely dependent on the elements. Indeed, it was now in the hands of the gods that inhabited this high and wild place.

The lightning show continued unabated for what seemed like several hours, but was probably no longer than one (time flies when you're having fun but almost ceases when you are not). Occasionally the flashes and crashes of light were so close and so bright that I covered my eyes with my palms to keep from going blind. All I wanted to do during that dreadful period was endure long enough to see one more sunrise, experience one more morning, live one more day, smell one more wildflower, witness one more campfire and waterfall and rainbow and full moon and, yes, lightning storm.

From far away.

For it is only at moments like these when we most fully comprehend just how violent and fragile and temporary life is, and yet also how very precious, and exciting, and jaw-droppingly beautiful. Because this earthly existence is not a right, or guarantee, or something to be taken for granted.

It is a gift.

Eventually, as late night evolved into early morning, the lightning subsided, the rain let up, and the wind began to die. After awhile the only audible sounds were raindrops dripping from pine trees and the sporadic low rumble of distant thunder.

At first light I put on my soggy boots and ventured outside of the tent. Never before in my life was I so glad to see a faint greenish glow in the east, clearing skies, and the gleaming promise of a brand-spanking-new day. My desperate middle of night, middle of storm, middle of hell itself wish had been granted ...

Although camp was a muddy mess and everything was soaking wet, I had nothing but praise and appreciation for the encircling mountains and valleys, mesas and canyons, heaven and earth, indeed entire universe. All was suddenly perfect. For after darkness, there is light. After chaos, there is order. After nearby danger comes even closer comfort. And after the stupid mistake there ensues, hopefully, the important lesson learned.

Following a thorough saturation of Grand Mesa, the massive storm system had moved off across the Colorado River gorge and was now enveloping the Flat Tops Wilderness in a dark bluish blanket several thousand feet thick. I could see stars and planets above me, and a waxing ¾ moon lowering in the southwest. All was as quiet and calm as dawn on the first day of creation. Ever so slowly, the right border of the cloud mass began to radiate a resplendent golden-pink color. Soon the whole eastern horizon was glowing saffron yellow and pearl blue, illuminating the landscape in a luminescence reminiscent of Paradise, or Shangri-la, or Valhalla.

Call it nirvana incarnate.

When the very first rays of direct sunshine hit my humble home, everything exploded into a million sparkling diamonds, one for every droplet of rain resting serenely like little Buddhas on each leaf and stone and patch of lichen. I could scarcely believe my outrageous good fortune, and spent the next couple hours walking around in a trance through the woods and meadows examining my newly acquired trove of treasure.

As morning progressed I found myself immersed in a peaceful, gleeful, ecstatic mood while going about drying out camp, repairing the tent, and preparing breakfast. Each previously mundane chore became a distinct and joyous pleasure. The sunlight on my naked skin never felt finer, the sky never looked bluer, the air never smelled fresher, the food never tasted more delicious, the views never appeared more heavenly to my lightning-bedazzled eyes.

The larkspur were never purpler.

It was the kind of morning you are given once in a lifetime—if you're lucky—and usually only occurs after dodging a bullet, or in this case, a whole bunch of bullets. It was the sort of thing that makes you want to live your life better than you have ever lived before, an awakening reserved for a perfect day after a perilous night, and an eye-opening episode I sincerely hope to never experience a second time.

Because, you see, I am never going to camp anywhere near another cliff or high place with a name like Land's End ever again. I don't care if the experts at the Weather Channel predict that there will be no thunderstorms in the Rocky Mountains for the next seven days, I am not going to risk undergoing another heart-pounding, soul-stirring, life-changing event like that electrifying night up on Grand Mesa.

One of them is enough.

First Light

The sand is starting to sift, and consciousness beginning to form, as four almost-silent feet come announcing first light. Warm paws touch naked skin, and fur rubs against hair, as someone, or something, is telling me it is time to get up.

The human world is still fast asleep as I roll out of bed to join the animals of darkness, the spirits of night, the ethereal, magical, almost-not-there realm of the nocturnal. Because, you see, life is short, and we only get so many chances, only so few opportunities, to enjoy early morning alone. Alone with the cosmos.

Sleep when you're dead.

I leave the lights off and peer out the window into the blackness, the swirling, teeming, ecstatic blackness of late night on planet Earth. The clouds have begun to break up, and I spy several stars in the sky, including the brightest and most beautiful one of them all, the morning star Venus, just now rising above the horizon in the southeast. I look away for a moment, and when I return she is gone, hidden once again by the clouds.

Get it while you can.

I feed the cat in the kitchen, and the night is so calm I can hear her chewing the crunchy morsels all the way from the back room. "Be quiet when the earth is still," says Joan Baez, and so I do just that, listening closely to the silence, the utter and thus sacred silence, from whence all sound and music and voices evolve from. For only after listening to the stillness for long enough can you really sing. And only after the dark night of the soul can you truly and fully experience the light.

The first light.

In between sunset in the west and sunrise in the east comes twilight, then darkness, then middle of night, then twilight once again. The cosmic wheel rolls, the heavenly cycle spins, the blessed circle rotates in super slow motion, and only if you are patient will you witness the wondrous revolution of Mother Earth blissfully twirling her way through the endless bleak void. Only if you sit calmly, wait quietly, and see with the eyes that you were born with will you experience the whole spectrum of day and night, night and day, life and death, death and then life again. For without the one, there would most surely not be the other.

I step out the back door, into the cool night air, and behold first light beginning to glow serenely on the far horizon. Here it comes. First a faint blue glimmer. Then a slightly brighter, slightly greener shade of color, for which there is no word. Then a yellow-golden light, slowly spreading evenly across the sky. Now I hear the geese. Now I see the geese.

Dawn has begun.

Once again, ever so humbly, ever so majestically, dawn has commenced across the American West. As water flows in waking rivers, and blood flows in waking veins. As leaves rustle, and creatures stir. As pitch blackness becomes dark blueness, as indigo turns into turquoise, as stars change back into sky, another day is coming, another drama is beginning, another mystery is unfolding in the gray stone mountains and bare bones desert, in the sagebrush prairie and hush-hush forest, in the deep cool canyons and deserted ruins. Yet another morning is approaching, yet another sunrise is proclaiming that everyone who survived the night now has one more chance to join in with the ancient dance and live, truly live, one more day in the brilliant and precious light.

Before the coming night.

Because, you see, we live in a world of extremes, where the very best things in life, like dawn and dusk, occur exactly halfway in between the two ends of the dial, the two sides of the spinning wheel, the two outer limits of the ever-swinging pendulum. Where perfection exists, indeed thrives, right in the exact center in between the exact opposites …

In between color and white, and darkness and light. In between cold and hot, and dry and wet. Between north and south, and east and west. In between the fish swimming in the sea and the birds flying through the sky, and the clouds up above and the dirt down below. Between noon and midnight, midnight and noon. Between the core of this planet and the encircling moon. Between outer space and inner space, between a rock and a soft place, between civilized and wild, old age and a child, between the future and the past, the first breath and the last, between death and birth, heaven and earth, we live exactly halfway in between the two separate halves of the one and same universe, where opposites attract each other and dance in perfect harmony.

I sit in my garden chair and watch the morning come. All is glowing. All is tingling. All is alive.

Suddenly the cat jumps up on my lap (after making "first rounds"). Little claws cling gently as I scratch her jawline just right, and my precious reward is the softest purr, I am sure, that I will ever hear.

Yes, morning comes early at our place. For we both know that life is short, exceedingly short, and good friends, the very best of friends, should welcome each other back, back from the land of sleep, and into the new day that is now dawning.

The Land of Yonder

Did you "play with mirrors" when you were young and all alone in the bathroom? Specifically, did you ever arrange two of them in just such a way that by slightly turning the nonstationary mirror you could magically witness numerous images of yourself displayed in the wall mirror, one after another after another leading off around the corner into some unseeable realm? Were you strongly attracted to that place, and did you find yourself attempting to peer past the curve to the mysterious world that existed just beyond your line of sight, just beyond your reach, just beyond the mirrors?

If so, you were answering the oldest call of them all, the one that beckons us to travel over the hills and far away ...

At age seventeen I hit the road. For something told me, or someone warned me, ever since earliest consciousness that I would never be content in this life unless it was spent wandering and meandering, vagabonding and adventuring, seeking and hopefully finding what it is I am searching for in my oldest heart of hearts. As I roamed North America by thumb, via freight train, and on foot I noticed that my goal always seemed to be around the coming bend, or across the next mountain range, or beyond the far horizon. Each new stretch of highway, each new town, each new state and province and country cried out to me like the sirens of yore that have been promising to lead pilgrims to paradise ever since the first young man left family and familiar surroundings behind and set out on his own into the Great Unknown.

My unplanned, unscripted, zigzagging trips across the map, interspersed with winters working a wide variety of odd jobs, became the legs of a long and epic journey, the chapters in an ever-growing book, the stages of a vision quest that I knew, knew like mad would take me to that perfect somewhere, somewhere out there.

yonder: *at or in that indicated more or less distant place, usually within sight.*
—Webster's Collegiate Dictionary

Where does the helium balloon go when it ascends so high that it disappears into the sky? What happens to the sailors when their ship leaves the harbor and never returns? What does the lone astronaut experience after his final radio contact?

Taking this thought a step further, what do you suppose is going to happen to you? In this life, in the next one, and for the rest of eternity? Now we are getting down to brass tacks, and why not? This will be our only chance to do so.

Because, you see, the essence, the epitome, the apex of this existence is we are going to die. But in between now and the moment of our passing we have the possibility of figuring "it" out before we have to, before we have no choice but to learn our destiny in the blink of an eye. For the ultimate fate that awaits us, tantalizes us, and teases us just beyond our capacity for realization is exactly where we're headed. That illogical, intangible, invisible image of eternity that nevertheless attracts our mortal eyes and encourages them to try and peek around the corner of the curve that is forever curling out of sight, yet ever luring us further. That cosmic carrot on a stick that keeps us constantly striving to arrive at our destination, to make it to the final shore, to grab hold of that which is beyond grabbing, beyond measure, beyond comparison, even so far beyond our wildest imaginations that we can only conjure a tiny fraction of its glory.

Fear not, for the very thing that you need, that you long for, that you would die for, is blessedly inescapable. You couldn't avoid it if you wanted to.

So before you reach the end of the movie and the credits begin to roll, before you reach the end of the rainbow and discover the pot of gold, before you reach the absolute end of the road that lies just around the last bend of highway, be sure to enjoy the ride in between here and there. Appreciate this fabulous voyage, even as you draw ever closer each and every day to the other realm, the land up yonder, that mythical Shangri-la on the far side of the mountain, indeed, the place we come from.

The List

Somehow when I was quite young, the notion entered my head that I would not be around for long. Indeed, at about age four, while playing on the neighbor's front porch, I had a vision, of sorts, that told me to get my kicks early and often, because I would never grow old or even see the age of thirty. A gentle warning, or piece of advice perhaps, from the universe to "get it while you can." In other words, life is short.

Very short.

And so, during my late teens and twenties, I lived life to the max and even made a list of wild and wonderful "things to do" before I died. Then I went about doing them and crossing them off as I did.

Having now reached the ripe old age of fifty—half a century—I realize that my dark childhood vision did not come true, and here I am, middle-aged after all.

However, looking back over my still ongoing journey, I am not sorry to have received that ominous yet obviously false premonition. Nor do I regret behaving like a Viking with nine lives during my early years. Because, you see, without that youthful revelation, I would not have done so many wild things, gone to so many wild places, or run into so many wild people, the kind you only meet out there on the road.

I would never have crossed paths with Jane.

Autumn 1980. West coast of Oregon. Hitchhiking south on US Highway 101, after yet another wolf-circle exploration of North America. It was a sunny, crisp, sparkling-apple October morning, and the old Mamas and Papas song "Go Where You Wanna Go" was playing on the jukebox in my mind. As my ride was slowly but surely coming down the road …

Jane was a little old lady traveling around America in a 1972 Volkswagen camper van that she called "Goldie." Several years earlier her husband had died, and shortly after the funeral she decided she needed to "do something." So she moved out of her

170

nine-room house in Connecticut (the same house she'd been born in and had lived in most of her life), got rid of almost everything she owned, and hit the road.

With her mate gone, children grown, and home sold, Jane turned her life over to the whims of her soul and the pleasures of this planet. She began doing all of the things she'd always wanted to . do, but couldn't because of family and other responsibilities.

When Jane picked me up just outside of Lincoln City, she was cruising down the West Coast headed for Costa Rica to spend the winter. In the past few months she'd been to the Florida Keys, New England seaboard, and Canadian Rockies. She was interested in everything, everyone, and every place, and was having a ball. We became friends almost instantly.

Neither of us was in a hurry, so we spent the day leisurely rolling south along the Pacific Coast Highway. Jane, Goldie, and I stopped at a dozen or more spectacular spots to dig the unending beauty of Mother Nature. We saw deep, fjord-like inlets, soaring cliffs of orange cemented sand, trees formed into fantastic shapes by the wind, and huge boiling waves of aquamarine green and neon white. There were overlooks where we could see fifty miles or more of shoreline. There were sun-drenched golden beaches, tide pools full of exotic sea life, and crashing torrents of translucent water shooting high into the air. We stopped at Depoe Bay, Rockaway Beach, and Devil's Punchbowl. We visited Otter Creek Overlook, Cape Foulweather, and the Sea Lion Caves.

At one magnificent viewpoint looking west out over the ocean, Jane fixed lunch in the van on her propane stove, and we ate macaroni and cheese with salad. When the wind blew the lettuce off my plate, we laughed out loud like little children.

Onward down the coast we went, the otherworldly lovely Oregon coast. The fall weather could not have been finer. At several places I ran off to explore deserted coves and mysterious caves, to climb huge rocks high above the waves. Meanwhile, Jane looked for seashells and sand dollars, or rested near the van, enjoying the sunshine, the scenery, the heaven-like perfection of it all with a perpetual grin on her face.

Later on, when I asked her why she was not afraid to pick up a hitchhiker, especially a wild-haired hippie like me, she just smiled and said, "I could see you were okay." Jane then explained her personal philosophy, which contained equal parts of karma, the Golden Rule, and how "we create our own reality." She believed that we should help one another, savor each and every precious day, and live our lives just as well as we possibly can.

For example, in the previous years she had volunteered at a soup kitchen on skid row, helped clean up after a hurricane, and attended peace marches in Washington, DC. She had climbed mountains in Alaska, gone white-water rafting in Colorado, and been surfing in Mexico. With a beatific smile and a touch of pride in her voice, Jane told me how she'd spent a night in the Key West jail for "indecent exposure" and "sleeping in public."

Now she wanted to learn how to hang-glide!

Indeed, she also had a list, a list of "things to do" before she died, and her blue eyes sparkled as she read it to me.

"Life is short," she said. "Do the important things first, not last. Do them now, not later, because last and later usually never come."

I got out at Florence, and we bid each other a warm and fond farewell. Looking at Jane's face, glowing in the late afternoon sunlight, I saw a beautiful woman sixty-six years young—not sixty-six years old. Her parting smile will live in my memory forever.

As she and Goldie drove off down the highway, I grabbed my road journal and wrote this line: "Always be able to associate with angels."

I now have a very important task to take care of. Something about a new list.

And I'm burning daylight.

References

Jack Kerouac, The Scripture of the Golden Eternity. City Lights Books, 1994.

Excerpt(s) from *The Immense Journey: An Imaginative Naturalist Explores the Mysteries of Man and Nature* by Loren Eiseley, copyright © 1946, 1950, 1951, 1953, 1955, 1956, 1957 by Loren Eiseley. Used by permission of Random House, an imprint and division of Penguin Random House LLC. All rights reserved. Any third party use of this material, outside of this publication, is prohibited. Interested parties must apply directly to Penguin Random House LLC for permission.

Santoka Taneda, Mountain Tasting. Weatherhill, 1980.

Ted Nugent quote used by permission from Ted Nugent.

Excerpt(s) from *Awakenings* by Oliver Sacks, copyright © 1973, 1976, 1982, 1983, 1987, 1990 by Oliver Sacks. Used by permission of Vintage Books, an imprint of the Knopf Doubleday Publishing Group, a division of Penguin Random House LLC. All rights reserved.

Pamela M. Kircher, M.D., Love is the Link. Larson Publications, 1995.

Edward Abbey from The Nearby Faraway by David Petersen. Raven's Eye Press, 1997.

Dolores LaChapelle, Earth Wisdom. Finn Hill Arts, 1978.

Dolores LaChapelle, Deep Powder Snow. Kivaki Press, 1993.

Jim Morrison, The Lords and the New Creatures. A Touchstone Book published by Simon and Schuster, 1971.

Kilton Stewart, "Dream Theory in Malaya" from Psychological Perspectives, Taylor and Francis Group, 1972.

Neal Cassady quote used by permission from the Neal Cassady Estate.

About the Author

Photo by: John Marshall

Curt Melliger grew up in the very middle of America and left at age seventeen to see the rest of it. During and after his travels he worked a number of jobs including pearl diver, pool cleaner, garbage collector, door-to-door solicitor for the Polish Relief Fund, railroader, bridge builder, engine mechanic, apprentice lineman, night watchman, carpenter, custodian, and caregiver before discovering his true calling in 2004. Since then over eighty of his articles have appeared in a wide variety of magazines, newspapers, and literary journals including *Alaska, Bird Watcher's Digest, Catholic Digest, Chicken Soup for the Soul, Cribbage World, Mountain Gazette, New Mexico, Oregon Coast*, and *Snowy Egret*.

Heaven Here on Earth is Curt's first book and a new take on an ancient, almost forgotten subject: Access to the ultimate while still breathing.

He currently lives near Cortez, Colorado, where he spends his free time exploring the wild places.

PUBLISHING CREDITS OF CURT MELLIGER

Spring 2017

Alaska Magazine (feature story with photos and illustrations)

Bird Watcher's Digest

Catholic Digest

Celebrate Life

Chicken Soup for the Soul

Columbus Telegram

Cortez Journal

Cribbage World

Durango Herald

Durango Telegraph

Four Corners Free Press (columnist for several years)

Front Range Review

Glenwood Post

Living Magazine

Mountain Gazette (2 features, 1 essay, 7 poems)

New Mexico Magazine (cover story)

Oregon Coast

Shamrock News

Skipping Stones

Snowy Egret

84 articles since 2004. Copies available on request.

If you liked this book, you might also like:

Dancing Forever with Spirit
by Garnet Schulhauser
The Three Waves of Volunteers and the New Earth
by Dolores Cannon
Raising Our Vibrations
by Sherri Cortland
Feng Shui From the Inside, Out
by Victoria Pendragon
The Convoluted Universe, Book 1-4
by Dolores Cannon
Let's Get Natural with Herbs
by Debra Rayburn
Out of the Archives – Earth Changes
by Aron Abrahamsen

For more information about any of the above titles, soon to be released titles,
or other items in our catalog, write, phone or visit our website:
Ozark Mountain Publishing, Inc.
PO Box 754, Huntsville, AR 72740
479-738-2348
www.ozarkmt.com

Other Books by Ozark Mountain Publishing, Inc.

Dolores Cannon
A Soul Remembers Hiroshima
Between Death and Life
Conversations with Nostradamus,
    Volume I, II, III
The Convoluted Universe -Book One,
    Two, Three, Four, Five
The Custodians
Five Lives Remembered
Jesus and the Essenes
Keepers of the Garden
Legacy from the Stars
The Legend of Starcrash
The Search for Hidden Sacred Knowledge
They Walked with Jesus
The Three Waves of Volunteers and the
    New Earth
Aron Abrahamsen
Holiday in Heaven
Out of the Archives – Earth Changes
Justine Alessi & M. E. McMillan
Rebirth of the Oracle
Kathryn/Patrick Andries
Naked in Public
Kathryn Andries
The Big Desire
Dream Doctor
Soul Choices: Six Paths to Find Your Life
    Purpose
Soul Choices: Six Paths to Fulfilling
    Relationships
Patrick Andries
Owners Manual for the Mind
Dan Bird
Waking Up in the Spiritual Age
Julia Cannon
Soul Speak – The Language of Your Body
Ronald Chapman
Seeing True
Albert Cheung
The Emperor's Stargate
Jack Churchward
Lifting the Veil on the Lost Continent of
    Mu
The Stone Tablets of Mu
Sherri Cortland
Guide Group Fridays

Raising Our Vibrations for the New Age
Spiritual Tool Box
Windows of Opportunity
Cinnamon Crow
Chakra Zodiac Healing Oracle
Teen Oracle
Patrick De Haan
The Alien Handbook
Paulinne Delcour-Min
Spiritual Gold
Michael Dennis
Morning Coffee with God
God's Many Mansions
Arun & Sunanda Gandhi
The Forgotten Woman
Carolyn Greer Daly
Opening to Fullness of Spirit
Anita Holmes
Twidders
Victoria Hunt
Kiss the Wind
Diane Lewis
From Psychic to Soul
Donna Lynn
From Fear to Love
Maureen McGill
Baby It's You
Maureen McGill & Nola Davis
Live from the Other Side
Curt Melliger
Heaven Here on Earth
Henry Michaelson
And Jesus Said – A Conversation
Dennis Milner
Kosmos
Andy Myers
Not Your Average Angel Book
Guy Needler
Avoiding Karma
Beyond the Source – Book 1, Book 2
The Anne Dialogues
The History of God
The Origin Speaks
James Nussbaumer
And Then I Knew My Abundance
The Master of Everything
Mastering Your Own Spiritual Freedom

For more information about any of the above titles, soon to be released titles,
or other items in our catalog, write, phone or visit our website:
PO Box 754, Huntsville, AR 72740
479-738-2348/800-935-0045
www.ozarkmt.com

Other Books by Ozark Mountain Publishing, Inc.

Sherry O'Brian
Peaks and Valleys
Riet Okken
The Liberating Power of Emotions
Victor Parachin
Sit a Bit
Nikki Pattillo
A Spiritual Evolution
Children of the Stars
Rev. Grant H. Pealer
A Funny Thing Happened on the
    Way to Heaven
Worlds Beyond Death
Victoria Pendragon
Born Healers
Feng Shui from the Inside, Out
Sleep Magic
The Sleeping Phoenix
Michael Perlin
Fantastic Adventures in Metaphysics
Walter Pullen
Evolution of the Spirit
Debra Rayburn
Let's Get Natural with Herbs
Charmian Redwood
A New Earth Rising
Coming Home to Lemuria
David Rivinus
Always Dreaming
M. Don Schorn
Elder Gods of Antiquity
Legacy of the Elder Gods
Gardens of the Elder Gods
Reincarnation...Stepping Stones of Life
Garnet Schulhauser
Dance of Eternal Rapture

Dance of Heavenly Bliss
Dancing Forever with Spirit
Dancing on a Stamp
Annie Stillwater Gray
Education of a Guardian Angel
The Dawn Book
Work of a Guardian Angel
Blair Styra
Don't Change the Channel
Natalie Sudman
Application of Impossible Things
L.R. Sumpter
The Old is New
We Are the Creators
Janie Wells
Embracing the Human Journey
Payment for Passage
Dennis Wheatley/ Maria Wheatley
The Essential Dowsing Guide
Maria Wheatley
Druidic Soul Star Astrology
Jacquelyn Wiersma
The Zodiac Recipe
Sherry Wilde
The Forgotten Promise
Lyn Willmoth
A Small Book of Comfort
Stuart Wilson & Joanna Prentis
Atlantis and the New Consciousness
Beyond Limitations
The Essenes -Children of the Light
The Magdalene Version
Power of the Magdalene
Robert Winterhalter
The Healing Christ

For more information about any of the above titles, soon to be released titles,
or other items in our catalog, write, phone or visit our website:
PO Box 754, Huntsville, AR 72740
479-738-2348/800-935-0045
www.ozarkmt.com